Wheels to Wellbeing

Books by Lori Ann King

Come Back Strong
Balanced Wellness after Surgical Menopause

Transform
Building the Mindset to Change Your Body and Your Life

Courses by Lori Ann King

Balanced Wellness During Menopause

Books By Jim and Lori Ann King

Raging Love
An Athlete's Journey to Self-Validation and Purpose

Wheels to Wellbeing

**A PRACTICAL SELF-CARE GUIDE TO
LIVING A MORE BALANCED LIFE**

Lori Ann King

Gunnison Press
LAS CRUCES, NEW MEXICO

Lori Ann King/Gunnison Press
Email: info@loriannking.com
Website: www.LoriAnnKing.com

Copy editing by FirstEditing.com
Cover design by Gus Yoo
Cover Photo by William Morton

Ordering Information: Quantity sales. Special discounts are available on quantity purchases by corporations, associations, libraries, and others. For details, contact bulkorders@loriannking.com.

Library of Congress Control Number: 2021917863

Wheels to Wellbeing/ Lori Ann King. —1st ed.

ISBN 979-8-9855379-2-5

For Matthew

Contents

Acknowledgments

I acknowledge with love, gratitude, and kindness:

Jim. I believed in you and our love long before I met you. Thank you for the dancing, laughter, and road trips.

Thank you, Carolyn Rabiner for pointing me toward balanced wellness.

To my IsaBabes, thank you for your unconditional grace, love, and support.

Thank you, Nancy Ottinger, for your belief in my dreams long before I spoke them out loud. I cherish you and our friendship.

I thank my editor, Michael at First Editing.

To Gus Yoo, thank you for another beautiful cover design.

PART I

Introduction

IN 2015 AN UNEXPECTED SURGERY dropped me into sudden surgical menopause. In addition to recovering from anesthesia and major surgery, I also had to navigate unfamiliar territory that I was not prepared for. I had no time to adjust to the difference in my hormone levels that came from the removal of my ovaries, and I suddenly felt off balance in my body and life.

Up until that time, my life had been lived at 180 miles per hour. I worked hard and I played hard. I believed I could live on minimal sleep. Yoga and meditation? That was too mild for me.

Then, surgery took me down. Surgical menopause was like running into a brick wall. I was stopped in my tracks, forced to rest. This was a good thing, but it was easier said than done.

In the months after, I tried, failed, and tried again to find balance. I had to learn a new way of living. I had to learn how to rest. I had to create new habits and make lifestyle changes with a focus on self-care. I had to learn to set boundaries with others, manage my energy more than my time, and recognize what I needed in my life to feel calm and peaceful. I had to create a safe haven for myself to escape the angst in my heart and the chaos of the world. I had to reject the world's idea that busyness equals success. I had to learn to set priorities, say no to things that were not in alignment with my goals and values, while saying yes to things that filled me with passion and purpose.

It wasn't just surgery that I learned balance and self-care from. My expertise comes from life experience, my own as well as that of those close to me. If you look for them, you can find life lessons from divorce, disappointments, failures, abuse, injuries, surgeries, illness, major moves and job changes, global pandemics, religion, sports, love, politics, and the death of a loved one, as well as the death of a dream. You can choose to learn from these situations and find a path to success. Knowing yourself and understanding what it means to be an extrovert, introvert, highly sensitive person (HSP), or empath can be enlightening, as can recognizing what causes angst in your heart and soul. You just have to dig deep to find the lessons to improve the quality of your life and create more balance.

I believe that no matter how dark the night, joy comes in the morning, whether that joy comes tomorrow, or some morning in the future. Bad things always have a time limit. And while it is sometimes hard to find the purpose in challenges or traumas, I believe that things that stem from harm can be used for good. With every obstacle or setback, you can change your perspective and ask yourself, "How can I prevent this from happening again in my own life or the life of others? How can I show more compassion to people? How can I inspire others?"

You might be asking yourself, "Do we really need another wellness or self-help book?" It's true, I've read many, and it seems like they are all saying the same thing. But I keep reading until I have my "Aha!" moment, until I find a book and an author at the right time in my life when I can truly hear their words and their meaning. Suddenly, their perspective changes my world for the better.

This book is about self-care, wellness, and wellbeing as seen through my eyes, my lens, my perspective. It's an exploration that comes from layers upon layers of life. It is about my transformation from unbalanced, chaotic, and overwhelmed to a more balanced, calm and happy existence. I hope that it is a fresh perspective that resonates with your heart and soul.

Chapter 1: Superwoman to Superhuman

Many of you are living life at Mach 3 speed. You fill your calendar from well before sunup to way past sundown, often working or simply "doing" into the wee hours of the night. You attempt to multi-task everything: your job, spouse, kids, parents, friendships, church, household chores, yardwork, groceries and meal preparations, checkbook, and workouts. You think you need to do it all, until you can't. And therein lies the difficulty. Because after all, you are human.

When asked, "How are you?" you reply, "Busy. My husband's busy. The kids are busy. We're just all so busy. I can't wait for things to slow down."

Sound familiar?

You are not alone. On days that you succeed at being Superwoman, you fall into bed physically exhausted but emotionally overstimulated. That's when your brain works overtime, criticizing you for the quality of time you were able to devote to each individual person and task, while at the same time jumping ahead to tomorrow and the rest of the week, hoping and praying that you don't forget anything and that nothing falls through the cracks.

You are constantly overwhelmed and on the edge of burnout. You no longer feel like Superwoman because you feel super-flawed. You stumble through your days hoping that tomorrow will be better, easier, slower. You need a respite from your hyper-connected life where it feels like you are always "on." You long for a break but don't feel empowered to give yourself permission to take one. The busier life gets, the more you begin to take shortcuts:

- "My job is so crazy this week. I'll just skip my morning prayer and meditation. I'll get back into it next week."
- "I'm too exhausted to cook tonight. I'll just grab some takeout. One unhealthy meal won't hurt us."
- "I'll skip my workout and stay late at work tonight so I can get ahead. I'll make it up next week."

Unfortunately, one shortcut or skip of something essential to your healthy mind, body, and spirit makes it easier to do again, and again, until suddenly your skipping of healthy habits becomes the norm instead of a once-in-a-while exception.

You also start neglecting yourself. "Self-care? What's that?" You reason:

- 'When the kids are older we can prioritize our relationship and enjoy date nights."
- "When the kids graduate I'll be able to focus on my hobby and my passions."
- "Self-care is selfish. There are just too many people in my life that need me."
- "I need to build my career first. After I'm established I'll make time for family and friends and for myself."

You wait until you hit rock bottom to slow down, set boundaries, and put your own needs first. Often it takes a crisis to get you to slow down— a death, divorce, an illness, or a global pandemic to cause you to pause, reassess, and reset. Sometimes your body slows you down, other times life brings you to an immediate and drastic halt. But you don't have to wait for a crisis to practice self-care and find more balance in your life. You can release your need to be Superwoman and become the hero in your own life.

Here's the thing: if nothing changes, nothing changes. You have to decide to take the time to analyze, reprioritize, and balance your life, set boundaries, and deliberately choose to live your life more abundantly so that you can experience more calm and presence in your life. So that you can live your life on purpose, filled with passion, and in service to others. You can live a life of true health, love, laughter, and freedom—in your body, mind, and life. It will require deliberate action toward creating healthier habits and learning new tools to examine where your life has gotten so busy and off balance.

That's why I wrote this book: to help you look at your life differently so that you can go from Superwoman to superhuman and, in the process, develop the awareness and skills to enjoy a more balanced life.

Chapter 2: Health, Wellness, Wellbeing, and Homeostasis

Society's perspective and terminology when it comes to health and wellness has evolved over time, with a recent paradigm shift being toward wellbeing. While many of these terms are used interchangeably, there are subtle and important differences.

When you are *healthy*, you are free of illness or injury. It can refer to your mental or physical condition.

Wellness goes beyond the absence of illness, describing a state of health in which you have both the ability and the energy to do what you want in life with relative ease. While it changes throughout the many seasons of your life, it is supported through your habits of nutrition, physical activity, sleep, and stress reduction. It is more than a state of health where you are free of illness or injury. It is a state of wellbeing that is the result of deliberate effort. Wellness has its roots in alternative medicine and at its core it identifies the whole person as a collaboration of mind, body, and spirit.

Wellbeing broadens the scope even further to describe a satisfaction with life that is characterized by health, happiness, and prosperity. It encompasses the joy you experience in your career, relationships, finances, physical being, and community or where you live. Wellbeing is living your life abundantly in all areas, where you enjoy true health, love, laughter, and freedom. It is where you move beyond striving and surviving and decide to optimize your life so that you can truly thrive. It is where you let go of living life on autopilot in reactionary mode and start living with intention, on purpose. After all, you can eat healthy and work out every day, but have no friends outside of the gym. You can have a beautiful relationship and a truly great love but dread going to work every day. These issues can increase your stress levels, reduce your happiness, and affect your emotional and even physical health.

That's where *homeostasis* comes in. Homeostasis is the epitome of the mind–body–spirit connection. It is a state of wellbeing that is characterized by peak physical, mental, and emotional functioning. It is the ability to return to a state of stability after an unusual or disturbing stimulus or tension has threatened your equilibrium.

As humans, we crave homeostasis. We long for the feeling that we are moving through life with passion, purpose, and control instead of on autopilot surrounded by apathy and chaos. We long to live our life with intention, on purpose, instead of in a constant state of reacting and adjusting to external stimuli.

The good news is, your body and mind are good at restoring homeostasis. They have built-in self-regulators to restore balance. The body truly is a self-repairing miracle.

Until it's not.

If you remain on autopilot for too long, caught up in the busyness of life, ignoring your nutritional, physical, spiritual, relational, emotional, social, and financial needs, then you will find yourself in a state of stress that threatens to disturb your overall sense of balance and homeostasis.

You may be thinking that in today's world, stress is inevitable. However, you have more control over your stress levels than you may believe. Stress is indeed preventable. It is simply the result of your daily decisions and habits. The number of hours you sleep, what and when you eat, the amount of alcohol and caffeine you consume, the number of hours you are willing to work, what you listen to, watch, and read, and even how often you take a break or vacation all contribute to your stress levels, and all have the ability to throw you off balance.

Regardless of which term resonates with you, health, wellness, wellbeing, and homeostasis are all moving targets. They are a balancing act, much like riding a bicycle.

Chapter 3: Bicycle Wheel Analogy

In 2014 my husband Jim and I began attending the Albany Campus of Life.Church. We attended The Chazown Experience, created by Craig Groeschel and outlined in his book, *Chazown: Define Your Vision. Pursue Your Passion. Live Your Life on Purpose.* Groeschel identifies the five spokes of Chazown,[1] or the fundamentals in life as:

- your relationship with God
- your relationship with people
- your financial health
- your physical health
- your life's work

As a road cyclist, this made complete sense to me and painted a vivid visual. I took this analogy and applied it to wellbeing, expanding it as a self-help tool to prioritize relationships and to reflect on and assess aspects of your life so that you can keep moving forward, maintain your balance in good times and find your way back during challenges or setbacks. *Wheels to Wellbeing* is a practical self-care guide to living a more balanced life.

Chapter 4: Inner Hub Inner Circle

A bicycle is made up of two wheels, each composed of a tire, an inner tube, and the wheel itself. The wheel is composed of an inner hub and outer rim, which are connected by a series of spokes.

Think of the inner hub—the core, the center of your wheel or universe—as your inner circle. Your strength. Who does that comprise? God, your spouse, your children, and yourself are all worthy components. These are your intimate connections, the people you are closest to, who have your back and whom you can count on to always be there in times of need. It is those people who are dependent on you. It is the people who deserve the best of your energy. Your inner hub is smaller than your outer rim and has fewer people, typically less than five.

The inner hub and outer rim of your relationships are fluid and ever changing. When you are young, your parents might be part of your inner circle. As you marry or have kids of your own, they shift to your outer rim. Yet there may come a time when they are ill or aging, when they come back into your inner circle; or when you are in crisis and they move closer to the inner hub. In the case of a divorce, your spouse may shift to the outer rim, making room for a friend or other family member to shift into your inner circle. At different times in your life, people who were once part of your inner hub may need to be moved to your outer rim, either temporarily or permanently. Friends, co-workers, neighbors, and your congregation may also be part of this outer rim.

If you are not careful, some people who belong in your outer rim may creep into your inner hub, using up valuable time and energy and taking the place of those people, passions and self-care activities that you require or desire to be a priority. When life is going smoothly, you may have room in your inner circle for more people. But in challenging times or times of crisis, everything and everyone gets shifted to that outer hub, while you recalibrate and find your balance, so you don't crash.

My oldest and dearest friend has a daughter who has bipolar disorder. Mackenzie was first diagnosed after a manic episode landed her in a psychiatric emergency room. In those first few days, my friend fought fiercely to protect her daughter and only allowed visits with those trusted people of Mackenzie's inner circle. This included herself and four close friends who were critical to Mackenzie getting the help she needed and instrumental in her recovery.

Aunts, uncles, and grandparents were not allowed in. They remained on the outer rim until Mackenzie had returned to a base line and had stabilized. This was hard for the family to accept. But the reality was, everyone was dealing with their own fear, questions and lack of understanding, none of which would help Mackenzie. She was the priority. She needed to sort through her own emotions and feelings without the added weight of managing others, or trying to please others, or even taking care of others. Her only responsibility was to take care of herself and learn to manage her disease. It was not her job to educate the rest of the family or relieve their fear. That was on them.

When you are dealing with a crisis, other people's fear, criticism, and judgment are not allowed in your inner circle. Your inner circle is a center for love. Always be more willing to disappoint the outer rim than your inner hub.

Negative, confrontational, argumentative, toxic, cynical people— regardless of who they are, including family— can be overstimulating or even harmful to your emotional and mental health, and should always be shifted to the outer hub. Set boundaries and do whatever it takes to steer clear of them, go a different direction, or avoid them all together.

Chapter 5: The Spokes

Between the inner hub and outer rim of a bicycle wheel are the spokes. These spokes work together to support and evenly distribute the weight of the rider. On its own, a single spoke is easily bent. Put it together with its fellow spokes and it supports a great deal of weight without bending. When one spoke does bend or break, all the other spokes take on more of the load. The extra pressure makes every other spoke more vulnerable to failure. In addition, damaged spokes can cause punctures to the wheel or get caught in your frame, causing you to wobble, fall, or crash. Every single spoke matters.

In the book I co-authored with my husband, *Raging Love: An Athlete's Journey To Self-Validation and Purpose* (2022), Jim wrote about one such time when one of his spokes broke, literally:

> Then one Tuesday night, it happened. I was riding at 24 miles per hour (as seen later by my Garmin that went from 24 to 0 instantly). I was in a sharp turn when a front spoke blew out. It stopped my front wheel on a dime and over the handlebars, I plunged. I hit the ground, spun in the air, and watched, as if in a dream, as my bike flew in the air above me I spun and rolled and bumped across the pavement again, and again, and again.
>
> Somehow, I landed on my feet, sliding in my cleats to a stop as my bike flew into the field next to the course, oblivious to the racers in front of me. I immediately felt nauseous as I collapsed to the ground.

Lori, having been riding right on my wheel behind me, saw the whole thing. She arrived at my side, obviously shaken, and concerned. I took one look at her and said, "Take me to the emergency room."

The result of Jim's broken spoke was a crash. He suffered a dislocated shoulder, severely inflamed hip, and a contusion on his knee that continued to swell with each passing hour. There was over $1,400 worth of damage to his bike and helmet. Every day was painful just to get out of bed or walk to his car. Overall, it was close to twelve weeks before he felt comfortable in his body. Being a self-employed personal trainer, if he didn't work, he didn't get paid. One broken spoke had a ripple effect on his health, finances, and work.

In life, just like on a bike, it's important to keep your spokes in good working condition, so you can stay balanced and continue moving toward a life of health, wellness, wellbeing, and homeostasis. The goal is to optimize your spokes and keep moving forward with minimal bumps and disruptions, but also to have a tool to help you get up and move on with your life when obstacles do inevitably appear.

The spokes in my wellness wheel include exercise, nutrition, peace in my relationships (God, self, others), financial freedom, nature, rest, passion, purpose, and play, to name just a few. Together, they support my healthy lifestyle and my feeling of overall balance and wellbeing. When one of these areas or spokes is not working, all other areas are vulnerable.

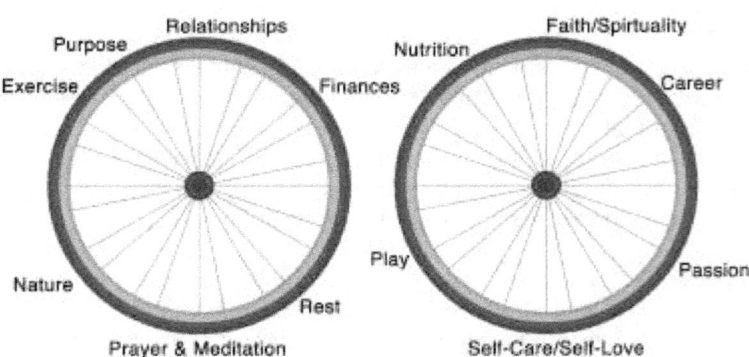

There have been times in my life when the spokes in my wheels to wellbeing were in pretty good condition. I was moving forward toward my goals and dreams with a sense of peace. Sure, at times one spoke or area would need a little extra attention. But in general, my ride of life was smooth.

Then there were other times—during my divorce, surgical menopause, and my husband's cancer diagnosis—when it felt like all my spokes were broken. Every single area of my life needed my attention. As I put each area of my life under a microscope, I dove into a world of self-discovery and awareness. I also began seeking solutions to regain my balance, so I could incorporate joy and peace.

Chapter 6: The Wheels to Wellbeing Tool

To stay as balanced as possible you need to keep all the spokes in your wheels to wellbeing in good working condition. Sometimes, some areas need a little bit more attention than others to stay balanced in life and health. For example, perhaps you've developed a healthy routine of exercise and movement, but your nutrition needs some tweaking. Or you have a great spiritual or love life but lack the connection of healthy friendships.

Wheels to Wellbeing is a tool to evaluate all the aspects of your life so that the money, time and energy you invest takes you further. It is a tool to check in with yourself, take inventory and determine what requires more of your attention. You can do this check-in on an annual, quarterly, monthly, weekly, daily or hourly basis simply by asking yourself, "How am I feeling physically? Emotionally? Spiritually? Relationally?"

From a reactive perspective, it is a tool to determine what is wrong when you are feeling angsty, irritable, or unsatisfied. From a proactive perspective, it is a tool to optimize your life so you have the maximum amount of peace, love, and happiness.

I believe you are capable of feeling much better than you do. And it doesn't (always) take a pill to make it happen. It requires a preventative and intentional approach.

The beauty of this tool is that changing one small thing can be a catalyst for improving your overall life. You start exercising and find yourself wanting to eat better. You improve your relationship with your partner and find that all your relationships are elevated. You go to work on your spiritual life and relationship with God and come to realize that your body is a temple, so you start eating better and exercising more.

When I got my nutrition right, my energy soared, exercise and physical movement came easier, and my fitness levels improved faster. Through a nutritional system a friend introduced me to, I ended up meeting more like-minded people, so I felt a better sense of community and belonging. Everyone I met within that community was an advocate for developing leaders and teams through personal development and growth, which led me to develop healthier emotions and a more positive mindset. So, you can start with one single step or focus on one single spoke, which at first improves one area of your life, but over time works as the stimulus for overlapping enhancements to your physical, mental, emotional, spiritual, or financial life. One small decision can have a ripple effect. One small change that improves the quality of your life and feeling of balance can be the catalyst for changing your entire life for the better.

Chapter 7: Your Specific Spokes

Think of the spokes on your wheels to wellbeing as the non-negotiable items in your life. What grounds you, fires you up, heals you, or supports you and your crazy life? What activities address your deepest needs?

Below is a list of ideas in no particular order. Rank them in the order of priority in your life at this point in time, today. Note that the order of importance can change annually, quarterly, seasonally, monthly, weekly, daily, or hourly. At any point in time, you can ask yourself, "What do I need?" Then, be still, get quiet, and listen.

____ Sleep (quantity and quality, including naps)
____ Exercise (cardiovascular, strength, flexibility)
____ Arts
____ Literature (including poetry, drama, story)
____ Visual, graphic, or plastic arts (painting, drawing, sculpture, design, modeling)
____ Decorative arts (enamelwork, furniture design, mosaic)
____ Performing arts (theater, dance, music)
____ Music (composition)
____ Architecture (interior design)
____ Knowing your purpose
____ Living with passion
____ Being in service to others
____ Massage, acupuncture, chiropractic care
____ Time with friends
____ Nutrition
____ A strong support network (counseling, psychiatry, women's / support group, writers' group, book club)
____ Socializing (weekly, monthly)
____ Date nights
____ Family dinners or quality time (immediate and extended family)
____ Faith / spirituality
____ Being outdoors (mountains, water, desert)
____ A satisfying career
____ Financial peace and / or freedom
____ Free time / spontaneity / adventure / play
____ Having a pet or taking care of an animal

Once you know the top priorities and non-negotiables on your wheels to wellbeing, you can begin to make time for each of them in your schedule. Over time, these areas of self-care that are meaningful to you become habits and you are less likely to neglect them. For example, cycling is one of my spokes and it has been ingrained into my schedule. At this season in my life, it is the first thing Jim and I do five days a week. Other seasons it has been three times a week and we had to work around job schedules and weather. My morning meal replacement protein shake, afternoon greens and adaptogens, evening dose of CBD oil and melatonin sleep spray, and my daily collagen elixir are additional self-care items that are built into my brain and my schedule. You may start every day with coffee or prayer and meditation, or perhaps you always have an essential oil diffuser close by. Yoga, massage, and girlfriend get-togethers are all components of a self-care practice that may already be part of your healthy routine.

Part II

Spokes That Keep You Balanced

THE FOLLOWING CHAPTERS DISCUSS some of the more common spokes and priorities that, if not cared for, can bend and break, causing your forward motion in life to feel wobbly and unbalanced. You can read through in order to get an overview of all the spokes you might want to consider in your wheels to wellbeing, or you can jump around in the order that applies to your life right now. Either way, I recommend reading through all the spokes that keep you balanced as a proactive way to intentionally address areas that need your attention.

Chapter 8: Move Your Body (Exercise)

The longer we go without exercise and movement, the easier it is to continue a sedentary life. Physics teaches us that the hardest part of getting any object—including ourselves—in motion is the beginning. But once we have created some momentum and made exercise a habit, we are in motion, and it is easier to continue in motion.

I've been active for as long as I can remember. As a child I was always running around the backyard, playing kickball, and riding my bike. In grade school I played community softball and water-skied with my family during the summer. In middle school soccer stole my heart, and in junior high I began running to stay in shape for soccer.

I ran through my teens, twenties, and thirties, then traded my running shoes for a clipless pedal-shoe combination and became a road cyclist. I eventually added bodybuilding for strength and yoga for flexibility and stress reduction.

Along the way, I did a lot of playing, trying new recreational pursuits including kayaking, rollerblading, hiking, kickboxing, swimming, mountain biking, TRX®, POUND®, and an assortment of fitness and cardio classes. Fitness should be a part of everyone's healthy lifestyle, but you have to find one that you truly enjoy in order to keep it consistent in your life.

Exercise may not be as familiar or habitual to you. That's okay. I encourage you to redefine exercise and live in your curiosity while you find a way to move your body in a way that you enjoy. The point is to find something you love, or at least like, so that you will look forward to doing it regularly instead of avoiding it like the plague.

Exercise includes cardiovascular, strength, and flexibility training, and each has unique and overlapping benefits toward overall wellness. Fitness experts recommend exercising aerobically three to five times per week for twenty to sixty minutes. Add in weight-bearing exercise two times a week, focusing on strengthening all major body parts. Flexibility can be accomplished through active stretching or yoga. This is the goal in wellness, but if you are just getting started, ease into it gradually. The first step is to start building healthy habits. There may be days when all you have the energy for is a five-minute walk. Do that. And do it every day, multiple times. Make it habitual, and every day or so, add another minute in duration.

A few benefits of cardiovascular or aerobic exercise include establishing or maintaining a healthy body weight, lowering blood pressure and bad (LDL and total) cholesterol while increasing good (HDL) cholesterol and insulin sensitivity. It can also improve your mood and increase your overall happiness through the production of feel-good painkillers called endorphins. Common examples include brisk walking, running, cycling, swimming, basketball, softball/baseball and football. You might also consider boxing, jumping rope, dancing, trampolining, hiking, rowing, volleyball, pickleball, belly dancing, aerial silks workouts, and hula-hooping.

According to the American Cancer Society, men and women of all ages can benefit from strength training. Strength training can increase muscle mass that decreases as you age, increase bone density and reduce the risk of fractures, help with joint flexibility and reduce arthritis symptoms, support weight control, and support flexibility and balance, which helps prevent falls and injuries. Examples of strength training include lifting weights and working with resistance bands as well as body-weight exercises such as push-ups, dips, sit-ups, lunges, and squats. Other movements that increase strength include stair climbing, hill walking, dance, digging, shoveling, Pilates, and yoga.

Flexibility exercise helps prevent injuries while improving posture, balance, and your state of mind. It can alleviate back pain and assist with range of motion. With greater flexibility you can experience less pain, more freedom of movement, and greater strength Reduced muscle soreness and improved relaxation of mind and body are additional benefits. Examples include stretching, yoga, tai chi and Pilates. Use of a foam roller and posture alignment exercises can also improve flexibility.

When I was first introduced to acupuncture, my local practitioner spoke to me about balance. My lifestyle had a lot of yang (active / masculine) energy. Yin (receptive / feminine), not so much. I had always been someone who pushed and strived through life, even in exercise and sports. I worked hard. I worked out hard. When my schedule overflowed, it was the yin activities, like yoga, that got dropped. My acupuncturist guided me to seek more balance. She taught me that I could be an elite athlete *and* I could listen to my body and seek harmony through counterbalancing activities, such as yoga, quiet walks, meditation, and qigong.

Some exercises, sports, and classes combine cardiovascular fitness, strength, and flexibility. TRX® workouts, Pilates, and yoga are a few examples. Plus, consider that yoga also strengthens your mind–body connection while its focus on breathwork boosts physical and mental wellbeing.

And let's not forget the martial arts, including karate, taekwondo, Krav Maga, aikido, jiujitsu, and kickboxing. Not only are these modalities full-body workouts, they can also increase your confidence and flexibility; improve your coordination, mental stamina, and social skills; lower your blood pressure and heart rate; help you develop self-discipline; teach you self-defense; and provide stress relief.

Exercise has always helped me to relieve stress and release excess energy. Cycling was and continues to be a tool that helps me manage stress and hormonal fluctuations. Strength training allows me to maintain and build lean muscle, which helps to speed up my metabolism, which helps with weight management. Yoga helps me to calm my body, which in turn, quiets my mind.

Above all, get creative and grab a buddy for support and accountability. I know a woman who, when she was recovering from surgery, joined a fitness class for older adults. She was the youngest in the group, but she made some great friends. She found the class to be just the right place to ease into fitness. The instructor was even able to provide modifications to movements in consideration of her post-surgery recovery.

Another friend joined an aerial and pole fitness class to spend quality time with her eighteen-year-old daughter. She met women of all ages with renewed confidence; pole fitness helped them feel sexy again. There is something graceful, captivating, and attractive about these forms of exercise. There are times in life when you just don't feel sexy. But there's no reason you can't feel good in your body and about your sexuality.

It is natural to feel intimidated when starting an exercise program. I find working with a personal trainer to be extremely helpful. Many trainers will offer introductory specials to help you get started and teach you exercises you can do on your own, while checking in with them periodically.

At different times in your life, you may need different forms of movement and release. Running and biking give me an outlet to burn excess energy. Playing soccer in my youth provided a healthy release from teenage angst in the form of kicking. Softball, baseball, hockey, and lacrosse allow you to throw shit, while boxing and football provide an outlet to hit people safely, with padding and protective gear. If you played these sports when you were younger, then you had a built-in self-care system to release negative emotions that you may have lost when you graduated high school or college. It may be time to re-examine a new modality that allows you to kick, punch, and throw things in a safe and healthy forum.

Exercise provides a daily time of release, meditation, fun and enjoyment. It can provide needed solitude after a highly interactive day, or camaraderie and a sense of belonging and teamwork. Many sports offer a place where you can use your voice to scream, grunt, and growl, sounds that are socially unacceptable in other settings. Outdoor sports and activities provide the added benefit of sunlight and being in nature.

Chapter 9: Hydrate Your Cells (Water)

Water is one of nature's most important nutrients. Every cell, tissue, and organ in your body utilizes water. It is necessary for digestion and absorption, it lubricates mucous membranes in the gastrointestinal and respiratory tracts, and it is the vehicle for many chemical reactions in the body, including metabolic reactions and energy production. Your daily intake of water helps to regulate body temperature, prevent infections, deliver nutrients to cells, remove waste, lubricate your joints, and keep organs functioning properly. It can also improve the quality of your sleep, mood, and brain functions.

If you lose more water than you take in, you can become dehydrated. Signs and symptoms of dehydration include dry mouth, lips, and eyes, as well as feeling thirsty, hungry, tired, dizzy or lightheaded. You may have dark yellow and strong-smelling pee and you may pee very little, fewer than four times a day.

For years I heard that the recommended intake of water should be eight 8-ounce glasses per day. But I always wondered why it wasn't different for a 120-pound woman compared to a 220-pound male. And what about physical exertion or working in extreme heat? Lyn-Genet Recitas, author of *The Plan: Eliminate the Surprising "Healthy" Foods That*

Are Making You Fat—and Lose Weight Fast offers the following recommendation for calculating your daily water requirements:[2]

- Divide your body weight in half. That is the base number of ounces you should be drinking daily.
- Cardiovascular exercise: For every 20 minutes, add 8 ounces.
- Strength training: For every 30 minutes, add 8 ounces.
- Alcohol: Add the equivalent of what you are consuming in alcohol. For every 6 ounces of wine, drink 6 additional ounces of water.
- Extreme conditions: Depending on the severity of heat and the length of exposure, add more water.
- Finish drinking by 7:30 p.m. to limit bathroom interruptions to your sleep, and to prevent it showing up the next day on the scale (if that is a concern for you).
- If you have limited bathroom breaks due to your work, then begin your day with 16 ounces when you wake up. Then drink 3 more pints spaced throughout the day. This will allow water to run through your system quicker so you can time your bathroom breaks. When you sip water all day, you may need a bathroom break every half hour.
- More is not better. Your water needs are based on your body mass. Too much and you can stress your kidneys.

One final word on hydration: thirst and hunger are interpreted by the same part of your brain. Clinical studies have shown that people often mistake hunger for thirst. To resolve this, engage a proactive schedule for drinking water according to the tips above, and eat consistently every few hours.

Chapter 10: Fuel Your Life (Nutrition)

I struggled with digestive issues for most of my twenties and thirties. Daily discomfort reduced the quality of my life and my overall sense of wellbeing. It was a spoke that was bent for years, and which took me years to fix.

Doctor after doctor told me that moving my bowels every few days was considered normal, even when I did not feel good most days of my life. I was eventually diagnosed with both diverticulosis and a type of chronic constipation called irritable bowel syndrome with constipation (IBS-C). My "gut feeling" and intuition was that relief would be found in my diet.

Under the care and guidance of an acupuncturist, I eventually discovered I had sensitivity to gluten. Removing this from my diet was a huge step in helping me feel better, with more regularity and less fatigue and abdominal pains.

Then in my early forties I developed a chronic case of idiopathic hives—"chronic" meaning I had them every single day for over five years; idiopathic meaning the doctors had no idea what was causing them. I was poked, prodded and questioned by dermatologists, allergists, and specialists to no avail. Eventually I stumbled on an allergy sensitivity test through a company called Everlywell. Through a simple at-home blood test I discovered a sensitivity to eggs and whey protein. I eliminated both, and not only did the hives go away, but so did the constipation.

As a way to live as healthy as possible, Jim and I eat organic as much, and as often, as we can. Organic foods are grown without pesticides, herbicides, and insecticides, which make it safer for the environment and to the body. Organic farming is kinder to animals.

One of the life lessons I learned from my dad is that food tastes best when you grow it yourself. I learned from my mom how to freeze, can, and preserve that food. If you have the time and energy to grow your own healthy organic food, you will save money in the long run while improving your health. So often, though, life gets busy. You may not have the time to grow or even prepare your own food. Based on the time and money you have at your disposal, do the best you can and make progress toward improving over time.

Jim and I also partner with an extraordinary health and wellness company that provides nutritional systems that work to fuel the body for athletics, weight loss, graceful aging, performance, energy, and an overall healthy lifestyle. Combined with great nutrition, we show people how to turn their everyday healthy food money into an income-producing asset. We offer nutrition backed by cutting-edge science guided by a scientific advisory board with third-party clinical studies. Our products are soy-free and gluten-free, with dairy-free options. Whether you follow a keto, paleo, 40/30/30, plant-based, Mediterranean, or alien lifestyle, our products and systems can fit into your diet and make living a healthy lifestyle simpler and easier.

Food is fuel. When I consider my active lifestyle, there is never a time when I'm not preparing for, performing, or recovering from a fitness or creative activity. Food is what fuels my body, my creativity and productivity, and essentially my life.

Food can be easy to digest or difficult for our individual bodies. And each body is different. What bothers me might not bother you. Stay curious and play detective, eliminating things temporarily if you are not feeling your best.

There are foods whose anti-inflammatory properties help our bodies heal. Food can be used to maintain or lose weight. Certain foods can minimize our symptoms of disease or illness while others, such as caffeine, sugar or alcohol, can exacerbate them.

In *Come Back Strong: Balanced Wellness after Surgical Menopause*, I wrote about the benefits of an anti-inflammatory diet. It's not just for menopausal women.

> *An anti-inflammatory diet is well balanced and something anyone can benefit from, but especially someone preparing for or recovering from surgery. Inflammation is the body's way to heal after trauma. It brings increased blood supply and nutrients to the affected body part and helps to fight off infection. Its sole purpose is to repair. So, in the short-term, inflammation is good. Long-term inflammation is what we want to avoid, as it starts to damage healthy tissue.*
>
> *There are two aspects to an anti-inflammatory diet.*
> 1. *Eat fruits, vegetables, whole grains, and fish*
> 2. *Avoid high-carb, low-fat foods*
>
> *Some top healing foods that will reduce inflammation and speed post-surgical healing include green leafy vegetables, bok choy, celery, beets, broccoli, blueberries, pineapple, salmon, bone broth, walnuts, coconut oil, chia seeds, flax seeds, turmeric, and ginger.*[3]
>
> *Foods that cause inflammation as they elevate insulin and glucose levels include flours, sugars, corn oil or peanut oil, pastries, cakes, and margarine.*
>
> *You don't have to sacrifice flavor by eating more anti-inflammatory foods. To avoid excess sugar and salt, experiment with flavor enhancers such as garlic, onion, ginger, turmeric, rosemary, cloves, nutmeg, and cayenne.*

Weight gain is a common complaint as you age. It can certainly throw you off balance or, at the very least, cause you to lose confidence. As a wellness consultant, I know what to do to lose or maintain weight. Even so, I still gained weight with menopause and during stressful seasons, like when my husband and I moved across the country between a prostate cancer diagnosis and treatment for it.

Losing weight is not always easy, but it is possible, and it starts with nutrition. Above all, offer yourself grace, especially during times of great stress while working toward improving the consistent quality of your food intake. Here are a few tips to assist you with managing your weight and overall health:

- Drink more water.
- Eat smaller meals more often to maintain blood sugar levels.
- Eat more protein and less starchy or empty carbohydrates like breads, cookies, and pastries.
- Eat more vegetables. The more variety of colors, the wider the variety of nutrients.

- Flavor with herbs and spices instead of salt and sugar.
- Have a plan and eat on schedule to avoid emotional eating.
- Be prepared when out and about. Carry the necessities: water, healthy snacks and even a meal on the go, such as a high-quality protein shake or meal replacement bar.

Chapter 11: Monitor Your Hormones

From childhood through my early thirties, the focus of my health and wellbeing was on exercise. In my mid-thirties, nutrition became important to me. In my forties I recognized how big of a role hormones had always played in my health, physically and emotionally.

Growing up, it seemed like my friends and family members were unaffected by premenstrual syndrome (PMS). I was not as lucky. In the days before I got my period I was in physical pain from cramping, and the combination of fatigue and bloating added further discomfort. As a young teen, I didn't understand why I was so irritable, especially for no reason. I felt so out of control over my emotions. When I finally got my period, those symptoms abated, but I bled for seven to ten days. As the bleeding stopped, post-menstrual syndrome set in, bringing with it mood swings, anxiety, and an encore of irritability, abdominal cramping, and back pain. I had one brief week per month where I felt good.

In my twenties and thirties, I experienced ovarian cysts, fibroids, and heavy bleeding, sometimes lasting up to three weeks. The medical solution was to put me on birth control pills, a form of synthetic hormones, and eventually a uterine ablation, a surgical procedure that removes or destroys the endometrial lining of the uterus.

Hindsight is indeed 20/20. Endometriosis was discovered during surgery to remove an ovary and ovarian cyst, resulting in a full hysterectomy and oophorectomy. At 43, suddenly with no ovaries, I began my research on hormones and hormone therapy. There is a big difference between synthetic hormone replacement therapy (HRT) and bio-identical hormones (BHRT). I have chosen the latter and am grateful to my doctors for helping me through this somewhat gray area during surgical menopause.

HRT / BHRT commonly includes estrogen, progesterone, and testosterone, or some combination of the three. HRT / BHRT is used to replace or support the body's natural hormone levels. It is not just for menopause, nor is it exclusive to women. My friend Natalie improved her libido in her thirties by taking testosterone, and my friend Keith was prescribed estrogen to manage prostate cancer.

If you are struggling with PMS or are in some stage of menopause (pre, peri, post, or surgical) you don't have to suffer. Whether you choose traditional hormone replacement therapy (HRT), bio-identical HRT or no hormone therapy at all boils down to a personal decision for you, your partner, and your doctors. OBGYNs, internists, family practitioners, endocrinologists, hormone specialists, naturopaths, and acupuncturists may be part of your team of support that helps you to make those decisions.

Men can also suffer from hormone imbalances and benefit from HRT. Symptoms of hormone imbalance in men include:[4]

- low energy or mood;
- inability to sleep;
- weight gain;
- brain fog;
- loss of muscle mass;
- low mood;
- anxiousness;
- acne;
- unstable blood sugar;
- low blood pressure;
- decreased sexual performance or low libido.

If you choose to balance your hormones, know that hormone replacement therapy is a combination of art and science. The science part comes in the testing (blood or saliva) of your hormone levels—your estrogen, progesterone, testosterone, thyroid, and cortisol. The art part comes in listening to your symptoms, and understanding what your body is trying to tell you. My blood work and lab results may come back showing normal levels, but I want to feel better than normal. I want to optimize my hormone levels and the overall quality of my life.

If you don't utilize HRT, then go to work on lifestyle changes and natural solutions that can help you improve the quality of your emotional and physical health. Assess and prioritize the spokes on your wheels to wellbeing to help find your balance.

Chapter 12: Sleep, Rest and Recover

"I'll sleep when I'm dead. Naps are for sissies."

That was my attitude prior to surgical menopause. But one of the symptoms I struggled with was insomnia. I couldn't fall asleep and I couldn't stay asleep. For me, one bad night's sleep leaves me cranky and emotional. My case of insomnia lasted for months on end, leading to fatigue, increased stress, lack of focus, and a zombie-like state.

When my friend's daughter was diagnosed with bipolar disorder, one of the first things they learned was the importance of consistent quality sleep to manage her condition. It is underrated and non-negotiable.

When you can't sleep or when you wake up fatigued, the typical response is to reach for a caffeinated drink. With months of poor sleep, I was no different. I took in massive amounts of caffeine and sugar to get through the day. Eventually, large amounts of caffeine made things worse, leaving me irritable, and adding to the disruption in my sleep cycle.

I experimented with many different things when trying to improve my sleep quality and quantity:

- **Evening rituals:** I keep the final hour or two before bedtime sacred. I turn off all electronics, including television, computer, and phone. As the sun goes down outside, I begin to dim the lights inside. I take a bath, read, or meditate.
- **Essential oils and tea:** Lavender essential oil helps me to relax, as does chamomile tea.
- **Melatonin sleep spray:** Melatonin is a hormone we produce naturally that helps us sleep, providing feelings of relaxation. When the levels are correct, it allows us to naturally rest at night and wake up with ease.
- **Supplements:** Magnesium is a supplement that is critical for regulating melatonin, and calcium is beneficial for undisturbed sleep.
- **Tart cherry juice:** Tart cherries assist with serotonin production, which is necessary for the body's natural production of melatonin. Other foods that do this include bananas, oats, tomatoes, and pineapple.
- **Swap television for reading:** An interesting fact I learned from John Gray, author of *Men Are from Mars, Women Are from Venus*, is that men relax in front of the television while women relax reading. It's how our brains are wired.
- **Acupressure mat:** Also known as a "bed of nails," I was pleasantly surprised how laying down on this foam mat with hundreds of short, sharp, plastic needles helped my body and mind relax so much that I was able to drift off to sleep.
- **Reduce or eliminate caffeine:** I began by eliminating caffeine after noon, then shifted it to 10 a.m., and eventually gave it up all together. Over time, I was able to add it back in, but it is the first thing I address and cut back on when my sleep quality or quantity begin to decline.
- **Naps:** I'm not naturally a napper, but I couldn't ignore my body's fatigue. Now when I hit afternoon fatigue or feel an energy crash, I listen and give my body what it needs, without guilt. It usually only takes twenty minutes and I wake up feeling refreshed.
- **Limit screen time:** After too many hours on my computer, my body feels the repercussions. An achy shoulder, tired eyes, and fatigue in my wrists means it is time for a break. And too much

time on my phone is just plain disrespectful to my husband and the people I am spending time with.

- **Progesterone:** For over six years I was on 100 mg of BHRT progesterone to help balance my hormones after surgical menopause. Then in 2021 my new doctor increased my dose to 200 mg. Suddenly, I slept like a rock, often in five- and six-hour stints. This alone drastically increased the quality and quantity of my sleep, and my overall sense of wellbeing.

There are times and seasons in life when more rest and recovery is required. After childbirth or surgery or following a traumatic or joyous event, your body requires more rest and sleep to heal and recover. As often as you can, allow yourself more grace for what is required: naps, quiet evenings, and mornings without pressure and a chance to snuggle into the covers.

When your body is tired and your spirit is weary, the best thing you can do is rest. Signs that indicate you may need more sleep, rest and recovery include:

- difficulty waking up in the morning;
- requiring more stimulants (caffeine, sugar) to keep going;
- utilizing alcohol, sleeping pills, or other substances to wind down or fall asleep;
- exhibiting a shorter fuse than normal, especially with loved ones;
- lack of focus, creativity, or productivity;
- excessive tears or irritability.

To become more aware of what areas of life might need some extra attention, you can ask yourself the following questions:

- "Am I fueling my body with the proper nutrients?"
- "Am I sleeping enough? Do I require a nap?"
- "When was the last time I had a date night? Family day? Time with a friend?"
- "When was the last time I got lost in a good book or a movie?"
- "Can I give myself a creative outlet through writing, music, dance or art?"
- "Do I need to unplug from the computer, phone, or social media?"
- "Have I taken a day, weekend, or week off lately?"
- "Are my vacations becoming staycations, where I work so hard around the house that I have to go back to work to rest?"
- "Have I rejuvenated at the beach, by the lake or an ocean, in the mountains, or elsewhere in nature?'
- "When was the last time I laughed?'

● "Is my schedule too full? Where can I build in rest and recovery?"

Overall, listen to your body. During a hot yoga session, I started my Savasana (think total relaxation or corpse pose at the end) about 15 minutes early. My body just said it was time. So I listened.

Chapter 13: Seek Silence and Stillness

Many religions and spiritual practices have some version of prayer and meditation, or talking and listening to God or a higher power. Prayer is sometimes the easier part; it's common to ask for what you want. Listening takes a little more effort and practice.

On the days that I meditate I find I am less reactive and overwhelmed. My physical body feels more relaxed when my mind is calm. Meditation is a tool that helps me create balance and reduce stress. When my life gets hectic or when I am in some form of emotional or physical pain, I have discovered that I have a decision to make: I can listen to the noise, focus on the pain, and pay attention to the minutiae; or I can tune into the still small voice within me and listen for its guidance. I can learn to calm the chaos in my body and mind, which results in more peace and harmony in my life.

My meditation practice began with a daily fifteen-minute "sit." At first, the only goal was to keep my body still for the entire time. Stillness did not come easy for me. Stillness was uncomfortable. I felt unprotected and vulnerable. But I trusted the process and the practice knowing that in stillness, I would grow, learn, and change. I learned to listen to the whisper that comes from inside, where God is. The outside world can get so busy and so loud; it's hard to hear the whisper. But over time, stillness became the place where I felt safe and grounded. It's where I made a deeper spiritual connection.

Meditation can also be practiced through making art or music, writing, coloring, and even gardening. Prayer and meditation can take place in a church, synagogue, house of worship or the great outdoors. But even good things like faith and spirituality require balance. There was a time when I attended church on Sunday, Life Group on Tuesday, mid-week service on Wednesday, Bible Study on Thursday, and prayer meetings on Saturday. In addition, I was rising hours before work for my own personal time of prayer and meditation, working a full-time job, exercising, and taking care of all the household chores and meal preparation. There were so many events and social gatherings to learn from and grow my faith, but this too required balance and moderation. I was not truly benefiting from all the spiritual activity when it was essentially leaving me overstimulated and exhausted.

In The Master Key System, Charles Haanel writes:

Over-work or over-play or over-bodily activity of any kind produces conditions of mental apathy and stagnation which makes it impossible to do the more important work which results in a realization of conscious power. We should, therefore, seek the Silence frequently. Power comes through repose; it is in the Silence that we can be still, and when we are still, we can think, and thought is the secret of all attainment.[5]

In the past, I would "run" through my day from the minute my feet hit the floor in the morning. This left me burnt out and frazzled. And the more tired I got, the less productive I became. By spending time daily, every morning, seeking the silence, I am refreshed. I have clarity, focus, higher energy, and increased productivity. I find I have more love for myself and others.

Whether you call it prayer or meditation or communing with God, it is important to learn to "be still." It is in the silence and stillness that your mind is renewed and your power restored.

If you are extroverted, then you may struggle more with the idea of silence and stillness. And if busyness is your form of coping or escaping or running away, then there may come a time when you are forced to realize that you can't outrun anything. All you can do is show up in the stillness. That's where grounding and healing happen. You practice silence so that when life gets chaotic, the inner stillness is familiar. In seasons of deep transformation, trauma, or growth, silence will be your greatest guide, your anchor, and sacred space.

Chapter 14: Fight For a Great Love

All my life I believed deep in my heart and soul that a truly great love existed. One of adoration and respect, where two people could walk through life as equal partners, recognizing and encouraging each other's strengths while filling in for each other's weaknesses. I was thirty-seven when I found it.

To this day, when I walk into a room, Jim's face lights up, letting me know he's thrilled to see me. With him I feel love. Adoration. Peace. Calm. Confidence. Excitement. Laughter. Freedom. Wild. Safe. Whole. Unbroken. Unashamed. I am enveloped and drawn into his unconditional love. Something about Jim makes me grin foolishly. I just look at him and feel an immediate sense of deep ease. He is my superpower. With Jim, I feel like anything is possible.

Before I met Jim, I experienced the opposite.

When I walked into a room, he scowled, as if disgusted with me. I braced myself for his venom. I bristled with anxiety and fear.[1] With him I felt unsettled. Judged. Unworthy. Sad. Angry. Unloved. Disliked. Shame. Guilt. Broken. Unsafe. Daily I walked on eggshells around him. I was enveloped by his hate. His love was conditional and I was never enough.

The way one man looked at me made me cower and shrink in fear and shame. Another man looks at me and I stand tall like a giraffe, expanding in love and respect. Perhaps it is because of that contrast, that I most appreciate and believe in truly great love. It's a spoke on my wheels to wellbeing that I deliberately focus on and work to make sure it doesn't bend or break.

Jim is not someone who completes me; he is not the answer to my happiness. That comes from within. I am responsible for my own happiness. But as a good partner, he certainly enhances my life.

Your great love is out there too. It may already be part of your life or it may not. Get still. Get quiet. Turn inward. Your great love may show up in romance, friendship or within your family. It may be with your pet, God, or yourself.

In your great love you:
- communicate your needs, wants, and desires clearly;
- work together as a team;
- refuse to talk negatively about each other;
- keep your promises and do what you said you'd do;
- resolve conflict and confusion quickly.

A great love takes great communication. Jim has often told me he can't read my mind. If I want something, I need to ask for it. If he can give it to me or do it for me, he gladly will, just to see me smile, make me laugh, increase my happiness or make life easier for me. If he can't, he'll help me figure out a way to get my needs, wants, and desires met.

Which goes hand in hand with working as a team. There are times we work side by side, cleaning the house, driving across the country, or

---

[1] Note: Everyone deserves healthy relationships. If you are questioning whether or not you are in a toxic or abusive relationship, get help, especially if there are children involved. Leaving may be the healthiest thing you can model to your child. If you are struggling with divorce and are still connected to your ex through your children, keep moving forward. Release the goal of winning or changing them and live your life as the best version of you, modeling what healthy self-care and balance looks like.

To get help, identify abuse, create a plan for safety, or help others, visit the National Domestic Violence Hotline at https://www.thehotline.org, call 1.800.799.SAFE (7233), or text "START" to 88788. They will even provide advice on how to clear your browser history or communicate with them in a way that keeps you and / or your children safe.

writing a book. Other times, we divide and conquer, going our separate ways temporarily to get things done individually. Either way, we both know the other is doing their part. This builds trust and that sense of teamwork.

You won't hear either one of us talking negatively about the other. Not with friends, not with family. We know that if we do, sooner or later, we'll start to believe the bad, instead of focusing on the good. And that will cause our spokes to bend or break.

When one of us says we'll do something, we do it. If Jim says he's going to pay the eclectic bill, I trust him to do it. If I say I'm going to pick up a package for him at the post office, he trusts me to do it. If for some reason we don't do what we said we would do, it doesn't mean we are good or bad or that we behaved correctly or not, it simply means we are out of integrity. We then do what it takes to fix it.

If you don't currently have a great love in your life then this is the season for you to develop a great love for yourself (more on this in an upcoming section). It is an important spoke that will add strength to your wheels to wellbeing.

Chapter 15: Seek Peace in Relationships

I appreciate a great love, and with that, great peace in my relationships. I work hard at maintaining that peace, knowing that if I do, it brings great joy. I believe one of the greatest joys of life comes from who you love. It's also where you have the greatest opportunity to learn.

Whether it's your partner, children, parents, extended family, friends, co-workers, neighbors, church, community, or yourself, love is a decision and an action, not simply a feeling. It is also done with intention. Like anything, if you neglect the important relationships in your life, especially those in your inner hub, you may wake up one day and find they are gone.

Relationships require regular care and attention. You are missing out on an opportunity to optimize your relationships if you do not nurture them. Friendships have a big impact on our psychological wellbeing.

Every relationship requires a different kind of love. Some value your quality time. Think of a child who just wants you to show up for their soccer game, and be present, not on your phone the entire time. Others, like your spouse, may just want you to be a part of the team: show up, roll your sleeves up, and get to work with them, by their side.

We all have limited time and energy. So you may have to get creative. You may have to squeeze things into the pockets of your life or you may need to rearrange your schedule. Your spouse may appreciate a weekly coffee date, whereas your best friend would love it if you met her at a BODYCOMBAT fitness class. Your mum wants weekly Sunday dinners while your dad would love you to ask him for help planting your garden.

The bottom line: don't neglect a relationship just because you can't give them hours of your time. They may appreciate a ten-minute phone call, a text to let them know you are thinking about them, or an old-fashioned snail-mail greeting card.

Occasionally, relationships require resolution and forgiveness. One time, a friend and mentor made a passive aggressive criticism of me in front of a group. She said something like, "Oh Lori doesn't need help with organization. She's got that all figured out." It was on a Zoom call and I remember hanging up and thinking, *Huh. I wonder what she meant by that? I do pride myself in being organized but I'm also open to learning new tools and tricks.* But her comment felt snarky and sarcastic. Something about it stung. I could have very easily drawn my own conclusions, wondered what I did wrong, or simply just put a wall up—which is my default—and let the relationship go. But she was someone I looked up to and respected. I chose to pause, take a breath, and call her back. I asked if she could clarify what she meant by her comment. What ensued was a beautiful intimate conversation. She revealed that she actually admired me for my organization. She knew as soon as the words had left her mouth that they had the wrong tone and could have been received negatively. She apologized and we were able to move on. Today, we still collaborate and mastermind together, and our friendship continues to grow.

In another instance, a friend criticized me in front of a colleague, someone I admire and respect. The three of us are all writers, and my colleague was telling us how she had just finished a 30-day challenge to write 50k words. She completed the challenge, but now the hard part had begun: editing and making sense of that messy first draft. Instead of commenting that all first drafts suck or about her own work, my friend decided to throw me under the bus and laugh about how awful the first draft of my first book was. Apparently it was so bad, she couldn't even make sense of it.

In hindsight, I probably didn't need to take it so personally. But I did. I could have called her on it, and let her know her words hurt. But I didn't. To this day, the friendship is severed. It was never repaired. And she probably has no idea why (until now).

The moral of this story is, it's up to me to communicate, to use my words when someone hurts me. As long as I hold onto anger, I'm a victim. I'm the one with the issue. To heal and move on, I need to resolve and release my anger and hurt, and find a way to make peace and move on. And maybe even learn to laugh at myself and not take myself so seriously.

There are other times when a relationship is toxic; when being around someone feels painful and destructive. It may even be abusive. And it may be a relationship that you are tied to by blood or marriage.

Not every relationship that is toxic is abusive. If someone is overly negative or critical or opinionated, you may find that overstimulating.

You may walk away from every interaction with them feeling angry, depressed or irritable. If this is the case, consider how you can spend less time with them. You can openly have a conversation with them, ask them to change and set boundaries on your time. You can also set a boundary on what you talk about. Growing up, my dad had a saying, "Religion, politics and affairs of the heart: three things we just don't talk about." While it was said as a joke, there were certainly friendships that were preserved because those topics were off limits. I realize some people thrive over confrontation and heated discussions or debates. As long as both parties enjoy them and those conversations are done with kindness and respect, then more power to you. Keep talking and debating.

Overall, you're not meant to go through life alone. Relationships are an important part of overall wellness. There are plenty of studies about the advantages to strong healthy relationships. The benefits of healthy relationship include:

- living longer;
- being able to deal with stress better;
- improved physical health;
- feeling richer;
- lower rates of depression;
- better immunity;
- improved blood pressure.

Your relationships can be the most rewarding aspect of your life, so whenever possible, seek peace and stay connected. Know who the important relationships are in your inner hub as well as your outer circle.

Finally, consider this: my favorite time of year is fall. Someone once asked me what my life expectancy was, and I thought 88 seems like a good number. Combine those two aspects and I have approximately 38 falls left (God willing). What will I do with those falls? What must I accomplish? Who must I see and spend time with?

How many falls does my husband have? My parents? My sister? The truth is, regardless of your age, you never truly know when your time on this earth will be up.

What if you were to treat every interaction with a loved one as if it was your last? Not from a mindset of fear, but one of presence and intention. One filled with love, support, and kindness. This will not only bring peace into your relationships, but a whole lot of joy, too.

Chapter 16: Give and Receive Support

Strong, healthy relationships are indeed beneficial. They provide support, encouragement, accountability, and a sense of belonging to a community.

During times of illness, a death in the family, or other crisis, people support you with food. It is human nature to want to help. People show up and feed you, often with a casserole. They comfort you. They offer you words of condolence and a shoulder to cry on. If you belong to a church, then someone is designated to organize a meal wagon. In some cities and towns there is a neighborhood welcome wagon, a happy and friendly way of greeting newcomers.

You may or may not have close family and friends during this season of your life. You may or may not be married or have a partner. I'm an independent introvert and very comfortable with a considerable amount of alone time. But during the Covid-19 crisis and pandemic, even I had too much alone time. I longed for connection. Add to the fact that we moved across the country to a city where we knew no one, and I quickly realized how isolated I had become.

I have to actively seek to maintain and create new relationships. I have one tribe of friends that connects weekly and sometimes daily on a video app called Marco Polo. I schedule Zoom and FaceTime calls with my parents and my sister, and I communicate via text and phone. At the time of this writing, I still miss some of the regular self-care rituals that connected me to other humans, including massages, haircuts, chiropractic care, acupuncture, reiki sessions, mani-pedis, monthly writing group meet ups, and wine and supper clubs with a few girlfriends. During the height of the pandemic, we still went in-person to buy groceries and at the very least, we were extra friendly to the cashier just for the in-person connection.

Being in a new place, with just Jim and I, is a great adventure. We both create our own schedule and enjoy time freedom. When our friends Abigail and William were driving home from Colorado to Florida, they drove through northern New Mexico. We drove a four-hour round trip to spend two hours with their family. Our friend Shauna passes through our neighbor city of El Paso every other month for her non-profit veterinary work in Mexico, and we make a point to share a day or at least a meal with her. While paddleboarding and kayaking in El Paso, we met new friends who love the water as much as we do. And when visiting a local coffee shop, we made two new friends simply by saying "Hi" and "I like your hair!" It's now become a regular informal coffee date where we show up and spend an hour together.

I know reaching out to people is not always easy. In the past, I was a private person, to the point where I didn't share much about my health challenges with my parents or sister before my hysterectomy. In hindsight, I could have done this differently. My sister would certainly have wanted to pray for me. My mom would have just wanted to be there, offering support and encouragement while preparing meals, doing laundry, and cleaning my toilets. Some days, that's just what a girl needs from her mum—particularly right after surgery when your body is using all your energy for healing its tissues.

One way to receive support is to ask for help. My friend Heidi knew a woman who had surgery and felt very alone. This woman needed assistance but did not know how to go about asking for help. Heidi suggested she utilize social media. If she wanted a turkey sandwich, she could post it on Facebook or tweet it on Twitter and have multiple offers within the hour. I love this idea. You could also ask for recommendations for people's favorite movie or book and invite some local friends over to watch with you or start a reading, writing, or coloring group.

Not everyone will know how to help you when you are ill or dealing with a crisis. This is where you need to communicate clearly by inviting friends, family, co-workers, and even neighbors into your life. Let them bring a meal, do the dishes or a load of laundry, vacuum the floors, clean the kitchen, or pick up a few groceries. They can loan you movies or books, or drive you to the doctor or pharmacy. If you have children, they may help with childcare or transportation to after school events and play dates.

Or, they can come for a visit. Some days you'll want to talk, some days you'll want just to sit. Ask for what you need and accept what they can give. Release them if they can't. They will be there for you another time.

Know that your friends are not therapists or counselors, and sometimes you require more support than they can give. I find talking to a counselor plays a large role in reducing my stress levels during particular challenging seasons of my life. They provide a non-judgmental listening ear and with their help, I'm able to feel balanced much sooner than if I choose to go it alone. You may need a therapist or a women's group, a prayer meeting, or perhaps a substance abuse or some other form of support group. If this is the case, ask your doctors, local minister, employers, and health insurance company what resources are available to you. If you are on Facebook, there are groups with like-minded or like-needed people from around the world for anything you can imagine. These groups can offer a safe place to discuss your fears and symptoms and ask questions.

Sometimes you are not the recipient of support but the giver. Through your life experience you can offer your knowledge and support to others. When I went through surgical menopause, I didn't know anyone else who was struggling like I was. I looked for books and support groups but at the time, couldn't find anything. There was a lot that I had to figure out on my own. Eventually, I began journaling and writing about my experience, and that was how my first book, *Come Back Strong*, came about. Through that book I've been able to connect to women all over the world as the giver of support and encouragement.

What I've learned from my own behavior as well as in talking with friends is that when we're hurting, we hide. We withdraw. We isolate. It could be that we've gained weight, we are in an unhappy marriage, our job gets crazy busy, or our child or parent needs more of our time than we are used to. This is when a support network is critical for helping you maintain or find your balance. And for those times when you are about to crash, a friend or acquaintance may recognize a bent or broken spoke before you do. Pay attention if someone tells you that you don't seem like yourself. Pause, and do an analysis of the spokes on your wheels to wellbeing.

Chapter 17: Prepare to Be Present

To honor and respect the people in my inner and outer hub, I do my best to live in the moment and give them my undivided attention. There was one particular instance that I knew ahead of time that I wanted to be one hundred percent present.

After *Come Back Strong* was published, it was time to celebrate. There were a lot of details to figure out, such as where did I want this event to happen? What day? What time? How to get the word out? What should I offer my guests? Coffee and tea? Beer and wine? How do I accommodate guests that love a good beer and others that prefer to cozy up with a hot beverage?

But there was one detail that I was absolutely clear about: I wanted to be fully present for my guests. I wanted to listen, laugh, and catch up for at least a few minutes with every single person that showed up to celebrate this milestone in my life.

I was reminded of a Bible story of two sisters: Martha, the worker bee, and Mary, the social butterfly. They invited Jesus and His disciples into their home, and Martha got pulled away by all the preparations in the kitchen. Meanwhile, Mary sat down with their guests, fully present, and able to enjoy their time together.

Now, as much as I want to be like Mary, the social butterfly, I know I am more like Martha, the worker bee. I pictured hosting the event in my home. I knew I would be in full-on Martha worker bee mode, and would not relax. I'd stress over every little detail, from wondering whether I had enough room for the number of guests I invited or the lack of fine dining. I'd drive myself and Jim crazy with the endless list of frivolous tasks that had to be done before the party. All while planning an event to celebrate a book about finding balance. When the day of the event arrived, I'd be busy bustling around filling drinks and snack bowls while picking up empty plates and napkins to get a jump on the cleanup. I'd focus so much on the preparations that I'd miss out on the most important thing: being present with my guests.

Hosting an event in your own home can be warm and intimate. But your friends aren't coming to spend time with your house. They don't care if it is spotless or pristine. They won't be bothered if you are in the middle of a remodeling project. You don't have to have a five-course meal or five different cookies for dessert. Many times, your friends won't even care if you feed them.

Your friends simply want *you*. All of you. Fully present. They want your time, your smile, your laughter. They want the twinkle in your eye, and they want to celebrate with you, whether it is the launching of a book, a marriage (or divorce), birth, graduation, holiday, or simply the fact that you opened your eyes today.

Here is what actually happened: I had our locally owned bar and bookstore host my party. They offer beer, hard cider, coffee and espresso, tea, as well as savory and sweet pies and pastries. Something for everyone. I got to be a little bit like Martha, the worker bee, and a lot like Mary, the social butterfly. In the weeks leading up to the event, I worked hard like Martha, preparing so that at the party, I could be present like Mary. I coordinated with the owners, over the day, time, snacks, and ordering of books. I got my invites out by snail mail, email, social media, and word of mouth.

And then, on the day of my book launch and signing party, for over two hours, I got to be like Mary, the master at being present, fully engaged with my guests.

The moral of the party? Prepare to be present. Do so with intention. Not only will the people in your inner hub and outer rim feel your undivided attention, it will strengthen the spokes on your entire wheels to wellbeing.

Chapter 18: Practice Self-Love

There have been times in life when I've felt guilt and shame over something I did or didn't do. I spent a lot of time beating myself up with everything I should have, could have, or shouldn't have done. There were times when I disliked myself more than I loved myself.

Many religions and spiritual traditions teach a version of the principles "Love thy neighbor as thyself." It's the premise of treating others the way we would want to be treated. The problem is, we don't love ourselves enough, which adds to our stress levels and bends or breaks our spokes.

Today, choose love, especially when it comes to yourself. Decide to love all of who you are... your past, history, flaws, misgivings, mistakes, weaknesses, and fears. In doing so, it allows you to love your present, future, blessings, victories, successes, strengths, dreams, and hopes.

When I walked away from a toxic, abusive relationship, I had to let go of my need to be a people pleaser, I had to get over my fear of hurting the man I was with, in order to save myself. I had to choose to love myself. And to love me, I had to leave.

One of my symptoms of surgical menopause was weight gain. It was frustrating, considering how hard I work to live a healthy life, only to have the number on the scale rise every month. At times, I hated my symptoms and my body—this wonderful miraculous body that had gotten me through surgery. But the last thing I or my body needed was hate.

Self-love is the act of taking care of yourself, your body and your emotional health. Self-love is showing respect for yourself and your wellbeing. Self-love is taking responsibility for your own happiness. Self-love is accepting and embracing the past, present, and future.

I love my body and all it's been through, even when it doesn't look or feel its best. I love the miracle that it can heal from trauma of major surgery. I recognize that I woke up this morning, and I am making positive progress toward true health and balanced wellness every day. There are some aspects of my body, emotions, and life that I don't always like. I love myself anyway. I love my future self, the person I am becoming, and the woman right now who is lovable just because she exists. She is more than enough.

Self-love does not always come easy for me. I find I can be highly critical of myself, instead of offering myself grace and forgiveness. My thoughts go something like this:

> *Lori, why did you do that? You're stupid. Who do you think you are? You are not good enough. You are not strong enough. You'll never be successful. You can't do anything right. If you showed the world the real Lori, no one would like you.*

If you can relate to this, then think of yourself as a child. A six year old. I call this part of me Lil Lori. When Lil Lori feels weak or scared, she gets critical of herself. She beats herself up. She pushes herself to exhaustion. The harder she is on herself, the harder she is on others, the more self-critical she is and the less fun she is to be around.

If Lil Lori were really a six-year-old child, my six-year-old child, would I ever berate her like this? Would I react to her with anger? Would I beat her up? Or would I wrap my arms around her and hold her, comforting her until she felt my love? Loving her until she felt safe?

While I am Lil Lori, I am still, at the same time, Parent Lori. And Parent Lori has the opportunity to turn things around and make a difference. To heal the hurt. To release the shame and feelings of unworthiness. Parent Lori has the opportunity to treat Lil Lori the way she needs and deserves to be treated: with love, respect, kindness and compassion.

Self-hate treats Lil Lori with anger, disgust, disappointment, and disapproval. This frightens and frustrates Lil Lori, making her feel unsafe.

Self-love treats Lil Lori with grace and acceptance. This makes her feel safe and free.

Self-hate has little respect for Lori's health, often filling her schedule with "to do's" until she is overwhelmed and exhausted.

Self-love gives Lori a time out. To rest. To nap. To color. To take a bath. To turn the phone or computer off. To go for a walk. To breathe.

Self-hate says, "I'm screwed up."

Self-love says, "I screwed up."

Self-hate says, "I'll never be happy, strong, successful, or prosperous."

Self-love says, "I am happy. I am strong. I am successful. I am prosperous."

Self-hate looks at Lori's thighs with disgust. "I have great abs, a lean upper body, but my thighs are fat."

Self-love looks at Lori's thighs and thanks God they are so strong and powerful. "They make me a great cyclist. The fact that my thighs are strong makes them beautiful. My thighs are a wonderful part of me. I am beautiful. All of me is beautiful."

Self-hate looks at Lori's tears and sees them as weakness or a lack of control of emotions.

Self-love sees tears as a source of compassion and the ultimate ability to connect to another human soul.

Self-hate blames, complains, holds grudges, whines, and criticizes.

Self-love forgives. Takes responsibility. Looks at the positive. Exhorts. Compliments. Encourages.

Self-hate is obsessed with the to-do list; you must be productive before you play.

Self-love plays first. Self-love colors, finger-paints, sings, and dances. It calls a friend. It watches a sunrise or sunset.

Self-hate feels shame.

Self-love offers grace.

Self-hate holds a grudge.

Self-love forgives.

Self-love, LOVES.

The danger of not loving yourself is that it can quickly turn into self-sabotage and cause more than one spoke to bend or break. Check this scenario out:

Your co-worker (spouse, mom, sister, teacher etc.) brings in leftover candy, dessert, or homemade cupcakes. You've been good for so long, really disciplined since the New Year. You've been eating right. Getting to the gym. Drinking your water and getting proper rest.

But, in a moment of weakness, after using so many "No's," Lil Lori decides to have one. One little. Itsy. Bitsy. Peanut butter cup. And not the organic, dark chocolate, raw almond butter kind, but the one filled with vegetable oil, loaded with sugar or artificial sweetener, and probably not an ounce of real chocolate or peanut butter for that matter.

And, maybe, just maybe, Lil Lori enjoyed it. Really enjoyed it.

Self-hate will beat Lil Lori up. It feels guilt and shame. It starts to self-sabotage. Lil Lori feels so bad that she decides to comfort herself. By having another peanut butter cup. And another. Until she finishes the entire bowl or the bag. By now, she's screwed up the entire day so she may as well keep going, right? Start fresh tomorrow. Or Monday. Or next month. Or after the holiday. Or next year.

Self-love goes something like this: Wow. I had a moment of weakness. I ate something outside of my plan for the day. It had a lot of sugar in it and it may cause an energy spike or sugar crash. But you know what? I'm not going to let one peanut butter cup take me down. I'm going to turn it around. Right here. Right now. I'm going to drink my water, eat the healthy food I had planned. Add a few extra minutes to my workout today, and tonight I'm going to get a great night's sleep. I'm going to hug myself. Forgive myself. Love myself. I am going to affirm that I am healthy and disciplined and on a journey toward being my best, healthiest, fittest, most balanced self. Tomorrow is a new day. I am healthy. I love myself. I love my body. I love Lil Lori. Lil Lori is pretty awesome.

And so are you.

Chapter 19: Enjoy the Comfort of Creatures

The word "Namaste" essentially means "I see the light in you and I reflect my light back to you." It is a mantra of peace and respect lived both on and off the yoga mat. In a world that has both light and darkness, love and fear, we have a choice of what we choose to see in others.

As a child and young adult, I lived most of my life anxious and frozen in fear of dogs. In fact, when a dog crossed my path, it felt more like "the darkness in me (my fear) sees the darkness in you."

My fears were not totally unfounded. I had several disturbing showdowns with canines. As a child when I was out selling Girl Scout cookies in my neighborhood, I slowly approached my neighbor's front door and reached up to ring the doorbell. Suddenly, a large German Shepherd came running out of the garage. My sister was able to run back out to the street, but I was trapped on the front porch, frozen in fear. The dog stood guard of its house, barking until my sister returned with my dad to distract him so I could get away.

Additionally, my grandmother had four small Boston Terriers that she kept tied up by the garage. Whenever we visited, they yapped incessantly and nipped at my heels as I walked by. They may have been small physically, but their bark was large enough to frighten me and have me running between the house and car.

As a teen and young adult, I was a runner. I came across many dogs that had wandered off their property. Some came out toward the road, barking ferociously. I knew they were defending their territory; however, I was always afraid they would break free of their leash. One time, one did.

On that particular day, I was out running when an Akita dog ran through an open gate of a fenced-in yard. I moved to the far side of the road, but he was too quick for me. He lunged and bit me, breaking the skin of my lower calf. The owner was nowhere to be found. I contacted the local health department, and it was recommended I report to the emergency room to begin a series of rabies shots.

These challenging experiences in my youth led to a fear of all dogs. Whenever any dog came close to me, I had an uncontrollable physical response of anxiety and concern. In my late forties, there was a huge shift. I had the opportunity to interact with several gentle, nonaggressive dogs.

One day, I attended a lunchtime reiki session. I lay down and covered myself with a blanket. I closed my eyes and began to relax. That's when I felt something settle in between my feet. I looked down just as the facilitator's small dog dropped his head on my leg. She looked so cozy. I decided there was no need to disturb her and we both relaxed into our midday meditation.

Another time, I was visiting a friend. As I sat on his couch, his dog jumped up, turned around twice, and sat down next to me, leaning into my side. She didn't jump on me, lick me, or bark. She just *leaned*. Surprisingly, I found that comforting, as we enjoyed an evening with friends together, side by side.

Then there was the time I met a man named Regan at a yard sale that I was co-hosting. He was new to the area and bought several pieces of furniture from me. To help him out, my husband and I delivered it. When we arrived at his house, the cutest dog came to the door.

"Don't worry, she's friendly," he said. I'd heard that before. But she was quiet and calm and I found myself drawn to her. Normally anxious around dogs, this one felt soothing to my soul.

As I reflected on my more recent experiences with dogs, I pondered over what had changed. What was different about these particular dogs? Were they calm, or was I? Then I remembered that several friends had recently told me that my voice was soothing. They said that they enjoyed my calm and peaceful vibe. Each time I hear this, I smile, fully receiving and embracing the compliment.

I realize it is not the dogs that changed. I changed. In my forties, I embraced the practice of yoga as a tool for self-care. Yoga not only helps to relax my physical body, but it also helps me to alleviate anxious thoughts. Yoga allows both my body and mind to gain and maintain a sense of calm and ease. I also began a daily practice of meditation. I experimented with reiki, qigong, and tai chi. These practices helped me feel calmer and less anxious. Nowadays, I share my light of calmness with others, and in turn, I see it in the people and animals that I meet.

Recently, I was out running errands. As I pulled into a parking spot, I looked over at the car next to me. Staring back at me from behind the windshield was the cutest little dog. His mouth was open, his ears were perked upward, and his tongue hung out. He turned his head to the side and nodded at me, almost as if to say, "Namaste."

You may not have ever had to deal with a fear of dogs. Dogs and animals in general can be extremely comforting and therapeutic. When a friend struggled with anxiety, her counselor suggested she consider a service or therapy dog. All sorts of animals, including dogs, cats, rabbits, birds, horses, and llamas, can be used for emotional support. They can be especially beneficial to patients with anxiety, depression, bipolar disorder, autism, ADHD, post-traumatic stress disorder (PTSD), Alzheimer's disease, and schizophrenia.

Growing up, I always had a cat. This was a built-in form of self-care that I wasn't even aware of. If I was sad, angry, anxious, or just wanted to be alone, I would retreat to my bedroom and close the door. But not before the family cat snuck into my room and curled up next to me. Somehow, she seemed tuned into my feelings, and her mere presence had a way of consoling and comforting me. Her purrs calmed my nerves and lowered the level of angst I felt during my teenage years. In your quest to live a more balanced life, remember how much comfort and joy the right pet can bring.

Chapter 20: Get Outside

Another built-in self-care tool from my childhood was the outdoors. Some of my earliest memories involve running barefoot through the backyard, playing kickball, and boating. Family vacations involved camping for a week every summer in the Adirondacks. It was a time before computers and cell phones. We always had a campsite right on the shoreline of the lake and there was a natural rhythm to our days. Most mornings I woke to my father brewing coffee and frying up potatoes from the night before into hash browns. Mom wasn't far behind, helping with eggs or pancakes. After breakfast we'd head out on our bikes, returning to the campsite to water ski. Next up was lunch, and an afternoon spent swimming, floating, canoeing, or skiing. The evening meal tasted extra delicious either because it was cooked outdoors or because we had worked up an appetite from playing all day. The perfect day came to a close with us all relaxing around the campfire. There were no to-do lists. Just play and rest. If it rained, we went into town to do laundry or we'd stick around the campsite and read or play cards.

I am still drawn to the silence, stillness, and sounds of nature; to fresh air and wide open, expansive spaces. My soul yearns to be near water— any kind of water: a lake, river, stream ocean, or waterfall. Swimming and boating seem to be a baptism that wash away the day's stresses and problems, bringing new life, hope, and possibilities. When I can't get to the water, sometimes a bubble bath can do wonders, too.

I also love the sky and mountains. Most days I can catch a sunrise, sunset or both. Living in New Mexico I'm able to ride my bike and hike year round. The daily dose of sunshine and vitamin D provides me with greater energy and vitality.

In 2021 I spent many mornings working at a table in my backyard before the heat forced me indoors. Just a laptop and my notes, no distractions and I could write for hours. Simply changing my location and workspace to the outdoors provided an added level of creativity and energy. My priorities reshuffle and I'm more aligned with my true nature when I'm immersed in nature. Getting outdoors as much as possible is a spoke that restores balance in a noisy, hectic world.

Chapter 21: Dance—Naked, If Possible

Dancing is not my first instinct, but it has come to the forefront at different times in my life. As a child it was ballet and jazz dance classes. In my twenties, plenty of energy was burned off on a Friday night at a local bar that had a jukebox.

These days, when my husband greets me with a warm embrace after a hard day's work, and slowly begins to sway with me, my worries melt away. When I hear him turn up the dance music in the office next to mine, I can't help but join him. We dance, smile, laugh, and enjoy the movement and the shift in energy and mood.

Dancing can be used to celebrate good news or to shake off a bad day. It shows up in my favorite tv shows, including *Grey's Anatomy* and *Ally McBeal*, and I can't help but join in when Quill or Groot get their groove on in *Guardians of the Galaxy*. It most definitely showed up in my book, *Come Back Strong:*

> Another way to change our negative feelings or energy is through singing, shouting, jumping, or dancing. One morning I thought I was home alone. I grabbed my iPhone and blared Nickelback while I danced, jumped, and bounced around the living room. I was energized and invigorated. I was truly dancing as if no one was watching because no one was. Until that is, Jim came around the corner. I'm not sure who was more surprised!
>
> Jim smiled with joy. I believed because I was dancing with glee and wild abandon.
>
> Then again, it could have been because I was naked.

Either way, it was a great way to start the day and a powerful lesson in being able to affect my feelings and emotions, as well as those of the people around me by simple movement.

Chapter 22: Take Time to Play

To play simply means to do something that is not to be taken seriously or to employ oneself in diversion, amusement, or recreation. It can mean "spontaneous activity" or "to move aimlessly about." Perhaps my favorite meaning is "free or unimpeded motion."

I have a Certificate of Advanced Study in Information Systems and Telecommunications Management from Syracuse University (SU). That's a mouthful. Many people have heard of SU and are impressed when I tell them the certificate is halfway to a graduate degree. I also have an Undergraduate Degree in Recreation from Western State College of Colorado, located in Gunnison, CO. You have probably never heard of Gunnison, unless you watch the Weather Channel and pay attention when they mention the coldest spot in the nation.

My graduate studies served me well. I was able to focus specifically on those courses that applied to my line of work in web development: information architecture, web site accessibility, database design, flash, and computer programming. I had a "serious career." But it is my undergraduate work that I'm drawn back to.

My early years working in the hospitality industry and specifically in recreation gave me the opportunity to remind people (and myself) of the importance of play. I could facilitate learning in an outdoor setting of hiking, boating, swimming or on a team-building or ropes course.

I remember hearing comments like, "Oh, you get paid to play," or "You went to school for that?" At the time, I took it as a criticism and thought people didn't take me seriously. I tried to defend it, claiming that there was a huge component of leadership, teamwork, and experiential learning to my degree. These days, I would view those comments as a compliment. After all, isn't the dream to do something you love so you'll never work a day in your life?

As kids we're told to, "Go outside and play." Schools around the world offer a period of "recess" where kids get to temporarily withdraw from their work. Why should we give this up just because we grow up?

Studies show that recreation
- helps people live longer;
- prolongs independent living for seniors;
- significantly reduces the risk of coronary heart disease and stroke;
- combats osteoporosis;
- improves self-esteem;

- increases creativity;
- enhances pleasure;
- reduces stress;
- increases life satisfaction.[6]

Just the fact that play can increase creativity and decrease stress is reason enough for me. Play should be an important spoke on everyone's wheels of wellbeing.

With that in mind, what do you do for fun? Where in your life do you purposefully waste time, where you have no purpose on purpose? Where can you spend the day in complete presence and simple fun? Where and when do you ditch the to-do list and forget goals and productivity? And who can you ditch it with?

As I reflect on these questions in my own life, I discover those areas where I lose track of time; where I'm not striving, I'm simply "being." In those times I am

- reading
- coloring
- writing
- riding my bike
- flying a kite
- gardening
- kayaking
- paddleboarding
- dancing

When I spend time simply having fun, I recognize that it's not my organization skills and productivity that make me unique. The engine that drives me is not the best part of me. The playful, fun, laughing heart-centered side is the best part of me. When my husband recognizes and comments that I'm smiling and laughing more, then I know I'm on the right track. Our days are meant for loving and learning and laughing, not constantly pushing and planning and producing.

In 2017, we lost my younger cousin after a long battle with brain cancer. I know she was a hard worker, but what I remember most about her is her laugh and playfulness. Even in her twenties and thirties, she was a kid at heart. I remember her as a young adult, kneeling on the floor over a coloring book, playing with my niece while the rest of the family was in the kitchen "adulting." She knew what was important.

Whether you color, draw, dance, paint, shoot baskets, water ski, or do cartwheels, take time to play weekly, if not daily. It will balance out the work and effort you put into the rest of your life, leaving you refreshed while increasing your energy, creativity, and productivity.

Chapter 23: Find a Creative Outlet

Growing up I would put the Lucky Charms™ cereal box in front of me and draw Lucky the Leprechaun by hand. In later years it was free-handed soccer balls and Tigger from *Winnie the Pooh*. I loved working with wood, creating sconces as gifts for my family. In high school I would have preferred to take five years of ceramics as opposed to three years of Spanish, even though Spanish would certainly serve me better today, living in southern New Mexico. I began my college career as an art major, but quickly decided I didn't know what I'd do with my degree. Not to mention, I really didn't have a lot of potential compared to the true artists in my class.

These days when I examine the spokes on my wheels of wellbeing, I look back to those situations and begin to explore if it's something that I want to bring into my life. During this particular season, the answer is no. I'm content to color by number on my phone. I find it relaxing and meditative. But every so often, it comes into my awareness and I know it won't be long before I have a season of creativity outside of writing. It may be ceramics, or paint-by-numbers or woodworking. Whatever it is, I know I don't have to be an expert to benefit from the creative and meditative outlet it provides.

Chapter 24: Laugh with Intention

Tiffany Haddish. Bea Arthur. Jerry Seinfeld. Queen Latifah. Betty White. Chris Rock. Carol Burnett. Eddie Murphy. Joan Rivers. Dave Chappelle. Lucille Ball. Robin Williams. Carol Burnett. Richard Pryor. Whoopi Goldberg. Wanda Sykes. George Carlin. Leslie Jones. Nicole Byer. Josh Blue. Kabir Singh.

These are just a few of the people who may have made you laugh over the years, depending on your age and generation. The saying "Laughter is the best medicine" is actually a Biblical proverb. A 2017 *Forbes* article listed "Six Science-Based Reasons Why Laughter Is the Best Medicine."[7] The author wrote that laughter is "a potent drug with the contagious power of a virus..." In addition, laughter

1. is a potent endorphin releaser;
2. contagiously forms social bonds;
3. fosters brain connectivity;
4. is central to relationships;
5. has an effect similar to antidepressants;
6. protects your heart.

Laughter is contagious as well as a strong antidote for a bad mood. It releases negativity in its path. It's hard to be sad or angry when we're laughing.

As part of a conscious plan to fill my mind and heart with all things of love, laughter, and fun, I seek ways to laugh more. When looking for a movie, I look for comedies. When I need a quick break from work, I search for funny YouTube videos. As I focus on laughter, I feel better. I'm not suggesting that you should never watch another serious or dramatic movie. But when your health, body, or emotions are compromised or you feel particularly off balance, then your body and soul can benefit from choosing to fill your life with positive and funny moments through movies, televisions, and books, or happy and inspiring posts on Pinterest and Instagram.

Chapter 25: Find Your Passion

If you don't already know what your passion is, you can discover it by living in your curiosity. Ideally you find a way to make a living doing what you love and are passionate about.

If you recognize that you are not passionate about your job, then you have a couple of options. You can go to work to change it, or you can accept all the positives that your job provides—the hours, the proximity to your home, the benefits, and the paycheck. If you choose to accept that your job pays the bills, even if you are not passionate about it, then pour your passion into other areas of your life outside of work, whether it's through sports or fitness, art, music, dance, service, or philanthropy. Choose to focus on what you can change, and accept what you cannot.

For me, one of the places I'm most happy is on my bike. Cycling was something I loved as a child and then detoured away from in my late teens and twenties. Rediscovering this passion in my thirties was like a rebirth. Just like when I was a kid, I love riding my bike. I love sprinting, pace lines, climbing up hills, flying down hills, seeing new places, traveling further than I could on two feet, pushing my body, and feeling both exhilarated and exhausted. Riding my bike in beautiful places is my heart's desire, and I get to do it with my best friend, Jim. Regardless of the circumstances of my life, if I can ride, then life is good.

So often, we stop dreaming. We forget our first loves. We give up on our passions. It could be due to time or money. It could be because life became about the struggle instead of the dream. It's time you gave yourself permission to dream. What was your passion as a child? Are you still doing it? If you don't know what it is, get quiet. Your mind, body, spirit, and emotion are connected internally and universally. You can't hear the still small voice pointing you in the right direction if you're busy, tense, or stressed.

Spend at least fifteen minutes daily in prayer or meditation. Buy a journal and write daily. Explore your past and remember points in your life you were most happy. What were you doing? Were you riding your bike? Gardening? Singing? Teaching? Working with your hands? Are you still doing it? If not, consider finding ways to bring it back into your life. My friend Willow loved to sing and act through high school and college. Then she got married, had kids, and somewhere along the line stopped singing. But in her thirties, she rekindled her passion. She found a local theater and now enjoys singing and acting there on a regular basis.

My friend Sierra is a runner who competed at the professional level in marathons and triathlons. As her children reached high school, she found purpose in coaching her son's cross-country running team, while continuing to indulge her own passion for running.

My friend Linda played soccer in high school and college. Now that she has three young kids, runs a photography business and is an active crossfitter, she finds time to play in a local soccer league where everyone's goal is to have fun while doing something they are passionate about.

Chapter 26: Discover Your Purpose

Jim and I are great together. We've even been called a power couple. We're also great by ourselves, we just choose to walk this earth side by side and many of our goals, dreams, and purposes overlap.

When he became a finalist and runner-up in a sixteen-week transformation challenge, I was writing my first book. He became an ambassador for healthy aging. I became an author. We each had our own identity. Our worlds still fit together and overlapped, and we were each other's biggest cheerleaders.

As you move toward midlife and beyond, you may find yourself lacking drive or motivation. You may find you have a heightened sense of longing for purpose. You reflect on the past with a strong desire to heal areas of stress, trauma, and confusion while at the same time you look to the future and ponder who you still want to be. You are searching for purpose.

When your life has purpose, you have unlimited energy and joy. Psychologist Shawn Achor, one of the world's leading experts on the connection between happiness and success, defines happiness as the "joy you feel moving toward your potential."[8]

Think of your purpose as a present, as in a gift. Ask yourself, "Am I withholding myself or my gifts from the world? Am I living small? Or am I sharing myself, my gifts, my talents, and my message with those around me? Am I shining my light so brightly that I give others permission to shine theirs?"

I didn't plan to be a writer. I didn't major in Creative Writing, Journalism, or English Lit. I spent close to three decades trying to work out what I wanted to do with my life. I went from job to job exploring, striving, learning, and always searching for that one perfect job where my gifts, talents, skills, passions, and purpose would fit.

Despite all the change one thing remains: I love to read and write. The combination of the two gives me insight I can't find anywhere else. I love the aha moments, the universal themes, and the life lessons that can be found in just about any situation, be it trauma, tragedy, or triumph.

This is probably why I became a nonfiction author. I write about universal truths that are illustrated by something deeply personal in my life. I dive deep into all kinds of experiences—abuse, divorce, surgery, surgical menopause, cancer, and racial tensions as well as cycling, the gym, food sensitivity, health transformations, road trips, setbacks and comebacks—and pull out the good, the bad, and the ugly. My goal is to add lightness and laughter to the world, to find the positive and hopefully inspire others to live a life of true health, love, laughter and freedom.

The summer of 2021 was a summer of writing. Many days I would write until I was exhausted. But each morning I woke up energized, invigorated, and ready to do the work. The work excited me. It was purposeful and intentional and it flowed with my schedule and energy. I enjoyed a morning bike ride, coffee, and errands with Jim, and then from 10 a.m. to 6 p.m. my ass was in a chair, writing. Writing is my love letter to the world. It's my way of sharing the stories that change my life.

You, too, have a purpose and a love story to share with the world, or at least with your inner hub. It may be through something creative like art, drawing, painting, watercolors, writing, music, or ceramics. It may be through sports, or teaching, or raising children. It may be in philanthropy, activism, or volunteer work. Take time to get in touch with your core desires and make intentional decisions toward your passions and purpose. They are critical, but too often neglected spokes on your wheels to wellbeing.

Chapter 27: Live in Service

The first time I took a road trip across the country it was by bus. I was 19 and scared. I did it anyway. My desire to go to Colorado was so strong. It was worth it.

I was transferring schools and, to convince my parents, I said I would pay my own way. The bus seemed like a good (cheap) option. It took two days and nights, and God only knows how many stops. At least one senior citizen and one snot-nosed kid fell asleep on my shoulder.

I arrived in Gunnison in the middle of the night. A student transported me to my dorm where I discovered, to my dismay, there was no toilet paper.

Up until this point, I had kept my cool and "warrior-ed" on. But no toilet paper? I lost it. I called my mom, 2,000 miles away in the middle of the night, sobbing. She calmed me down and told me there must be a gas station nearby where I could go get myself a roll. She was right.

That was August, and as we headed into November I realized I could not afford the plane ticket home for Thanksgiving. I asked around and learned that a lot of students stayed on campus. There was a local organization that provided a free Thanksgiving meal to college students as well as to members of the community. I decided to volunteer in an attempt to stay busy and connected.

That morning I peeled, chopped, and helped prepare the Thanksgiving feast. As people arrived, I greeted and served them with a smile. As lonely as I was, I had a great time. By volunteering, my focus shifted, off myself and my inability to be at home with loved ones, and on to the people that showed up, some of whom might not have eaten that day had we not provided a free meal.

It's easy to get caught up in yourself and your own small world and its many challenges and problems. When we volunteer or give back, we go from a "me" to a "we" mentality, something Jim wrote about in *Raging Love:*

> *A single-minded focus helped me succeed as an athlete, but winning competitions did not give me meaning, purpose, or direction. Sometimes it's more like an addiction like gambling with slot machines, no matter what the pain and suffering, you're one pull away from the ultimate success and happiness. It was when I shifted my focus from myself onto others and saw their joy in improving and performing at their best, my life became full of purpose, self-validation, and pride.... Ultimately, I found the most peace and happiness when I stepped off the ball competitively, and made my life more about assisting others in their journey.*

Chapter 28: Find Peace in Your Career

I grew up in the Finger Lakes region of Central NY. My dad was a truck driver who worked long hours, and often two or three jobs at a time. He was a hard worker. His belief was that your primary job paid the bills, and your overtime or second job paid for toys and fun.

My mom was a bookkeeper at a local grocery store. She worked from home as a Girl Scout Cookie mom, handling orders, warehousing, and distribution. She was a Tupperware lady and years later, in retirement, sold Avon. Tupperware pioneered the direct marketing strategy made famous by the Tupperware party. A Tupperware party was a collaboration between a Tupperware dealer and a host or hostess. The host or hostess invited friends, family members, and neighbors into their home where the dealer demonstrated and sold the products and led the group in party games. The host or hostess earned free products based on the amount of sales made at their party. The Tupperware party allowed for women to work and enjoy the benefits of earning an income while still keeping their focus on family and home.

I'm grateful for the work ethic that my dad taught me, and the entrepreneurial spirit—along with the belief you could earn an income from home—that my mom demonstrated to me.

For the first half of my career, I followed my dad's path. Multiple streams of income simply meant working multiple jobs. However, this often meant working seven days a week, evenings, weekends, and holidays. I traded time for money. My time was not my own. My money was not accumulating. If I didn't work, I didn't get paid. Plus, due to the stress and extreme hours, my health declined.

My many different jobs and careers were in recreation, marketing, and web development. In changing jobs every few years, I realized that I didn't actually want a job. I didn't want to work for someone else. I wanted to build. Create. Write. Inspire. I still have the same work ethic I was raised with, I just now apply it to my own passion and purpose.

I'm grateful for every single job I ever had. Each was an opportunity to be stronger and more courageous. And each one taught me a skill that I still use today. With every job change I made, I discovered that I personally work and feel better without a boss. I have a deep need to prove myself and please my supervisors. I long to be seen and recognized as a hard worker, efficient, organized, productive, able to keep all the balls in the air at the same time. But inevitably that leads me very quickly to burnout.

In 2009, a friend introduced me to a nutritional cleansing and replenishment system that transformed my health, improved my athletic performance, and gave me the athletic physique I had always wanted. It has also provided me with the opportunity to own my own business while working from home. Network marketing is an equal opportunity industry where the sky's the limit on what you can earn, as long as you have drive, determination, and perseverance.

Best of all, it introduced me to the concept of passive income. Passive income is money earned with little or no ongoing effort, but with an upfront investment of time and / or money. Once I discovered my passion and purpose as an author, I recognized that writing books and creating courses was an additional way to work smarter, not harder. Now as an authorpreneur, I'm able to make my own hours, rise without an alarm clock, and my work follows my energy, not the clock or the calendar.

This life is not for everyone. It has its risks. If you have never been exposed to an entrepreneurial or investor mindset, then it will require a lot of reading and personal development. For me, it is the ongoing belief that I am investing in myself and my family's future. I learn not by going back to school, but by doing the work and earning while I learn.

To find peace and happiness in my career, I had to give up life as an employee so I could be fully present to my purpose on this planet. I truly love my life as a writer and I know that loving one's work is a gift. But I had a lot to learn in moving from employee to business owner. I have learned that to be successful, sell books, and earn a living, I have to treat my writing as a business. One resource that helped me to move from an employee mindset to a business mindset is Robert T. Kiyosaki's book, *Rich Dad's CASHFLOW Quadrant: Rich Dad's Guide to Financial Freedom*. A resource that helped move my writing into a profitable business is Steve Pieper's Author Marketing Mastery through Optimization (AMMO) Program.

Whether you thrive as an employee, self-employed person, business owner or investor, you will spend over a third of your life working. Find a way to do it joyfully, or at least to be at peace with your career.

Chapter 29: Keep Growing

One of the best parts of my marriage is that both Jim and I are committed to self-development, learning, and growing. We seek balance and forward movement toward our dreams and bliss. So if personal growth and development is one of your spokes, it matters, because if it's bent or broken, then it makes all the other spokes vulnerable.

I'm going to stray from my bike analogy for a moment and share something I heard about the trees in a forest. While individual trees are what make up the whole of a forest, their roots are intertwined. Each tree stands tall and independent. But it's what's below the surface that counts. If one tree gets sick or diseased, because of those intertwined roots, it affects all the trees in the forest.

To keep my family whole and healthy, I have to pay attention to my own self-care and overall sense of balance in life, on a physical, emotional, and mental level. I do this with affirmations, journaling, and counseling as needed. I move my body, hydrate my cells, fuel my life and monitor my hormones. I pay attention to sleep, rest, and play. I focus on passion and purpose and serving others. I work hard to be my best self and keep growing for the benefit and health of my family, community, and world. These are the spokes on my wheels to wellbeing. If you haven't already done so, go back to the Introduction and chapter 7 called "Your Specific Spokes," and make a list of the important self-care practices and priorities in your life. Knowing what your spokes are is a key to living a more balanced life.

Part III

What Breaks Your Spokes

BENT AND BROKEN SPOKES, along with people who push their way from your outer hub into your inner circle, are inevitable. From these obstacles you learn compassion, kindness, and connection. You learn to set boundaries and recognize triggers so, hopefully, you can avoid the same difficulties happening again multiple times in your lifetime.

Triggers are anything and anybody that stress you out. Who brings you down or riles you up? Who or what pisses you off? What is the activity that pushes you into overwhelm and exhaustion?

I am acutely aware that crowds stress me out and send my anxiety through the roof. The last place I want to be on Black Friday is at a mall or shopping center. And while it's impossible to avoid large crowds at some of the annual events I attend, I now know myself and what I require to recalibrate and find my balance, which I'll discuss in a later section.

Are there foods that increase your stress or anxiety or fatigue? Life is hard enough without exposing yourself to smoke or excessive use of salt, sugar, caffeine, MSG, hydrogenated fats, drugs, and alcohol.

How about the weather? Do you live in the land of the concrete sky while dreaming of living in an area that gets over 300 days of sunshine per year?

Do you live your life waiting for Friday and dreading Monday?

In the following chapters, I'll point out a few specific obstacles that are common spoke benders and breakers.

Chapter 30: The Obstacles in a Riders Path

Just like when riding a bike, life throws obstacles in your path that disrupt the ease and flow of your ride. You're riding along, enjoying the smooth pavement below you, the sun and blue skies above you, and the wind in your face. All of a sudden, the road turns to dirt, gravel, or cobblestones.

Or you get a flat tire. Some obstacles you walk around and get back on the path quickly. Others, you have to turn around and go back the way you came, and find another route to get to where you want to go.

The obstacles on my life path have included divorce, marriage, moving, cancer diagnoses for my husband and both of my parents, changing jobs, surgery, and surgical menopause. The hazards on your path may be the death of a loved one or the death of a dream, bankruptcy, retirement, having a child or becoming an empty nester. Even good obstacles can throw you off balance or force you to lose your momentum.

When dealing with a traumatic obstacle, you will need time to heal. As the days and weeks pass by, you may struggle to regain your balance physically, emotionally, psychologically, socially, or even financially. You want to be free of physical pain and illness, but you also want to be healthy on a mental, emotional, financial, and social level.

There will be times when it feels as if one spoke is bent or broken. You can focus on repairing it individually. Other times, it feels like all your spokes are broken. Every single area of your life needs your attention. As you put each area of your life under a microscope, you have the opportunity to dive into a world of self-discovery and awareness. You will also seek solutions to regain your balance, so you can live with more joy and peace. Wellness indeed takes deliberate effort. Reclaiming homeostasis does not typically happen overnight, and even when it's been established, it continues to be an ongoing balancing act.

Chapter 31: Busyness

My strong work ethic sometimes crosses over into workaholism. But my endless ever-growing to-do list never makes me feel the way I want. It easily becomes an addiction. If I just complete enough on my list, I'll feel whole, proud, and happy. If I just get enough done I'll earn a rest or a play day. Unfortunately, the work is never done.

The more my to-do list grows, the more overwhelmed I feel, making me ineffective. So instead of prioritizing items on my list, I actually add things to it that I think I can get done quickly, just to make myself feel more productive. But that is a short-term emotional high, and I eventually end up feeling even more overwhelmed and ineffective.

Activity keeps me from feeling. It is numbing. When I am busy I can ignore my feelings of boredom or anxiety or sadness. I ignore my physical and emotional need for rest in order to try to prove I am a hard worker. Busyness makes me less able to connect to my own heart and to others. I drive and push and strive until at some point I reach exhaustion and it becomes too much. I become too fatigued to be productive or creative. My standards are too high even for me to meet.

So let me ask you: Are you busy?

Only you have the power to change it. Only you can decide that you want to be happy and rested instead of afraid, wired, or panicky. To choose grace and nourishment over exhaustion and starvation. It is counter-cultural—and slightly rebellious—to choose to be less busy, less overwhelmed, to build more quiet time into your schedule, and to slow down and be present.

Your greatness is not found in being busy, organized, and productive. It's found in the silly, playful, moments where you are quick to laugh and cry; when you are fully present, especially with those people in your inner hub.

When you and your family are so busy and so scheduled every minute of every day, you don't recognize when something is off. You become so focused on the busyness that you don't notice someone right in front of you that is hurting, even if that someone is you.

To break the addiction of busyness, learn to delegate. Team up with a friend or family member. Examine whether what you are doing is truly important. Say no. Cry out. Ask for help. You are not meant to do life alone.

Reread the "Inner Hub Inner Circle" and "Seek Silence and Stillness" chapters. Let go of everything you "should" do. Re-evaluate everything that causes you to be busy and make sure it's in alignment with your passion and purpose as well as a priority with the people in your inner hub.

Chapter 32: Jumping Back in Too Quickly

Immediately following my hysterectomy and oophorectomy, I was struggling both physically and emotionally, and I didn't know how to help myself feel better again. I didn't know how to regain my balance. I felt weak. I was out and about, attending a business meeting even though I felt awful. It hurt to walk, sit, and stand. I couldn't get comfortable. I had about an hour of energy to spare before I needed a nap.

Six weeks after surgery, I threw myself back into my life at full tilt. My mood swings and tired soul returned to work full-time. I traveled on weekends, worked a normal schedule, biked, went to the gym, attended Toastmasters meetings, and socialized with family and friends. Months after my surgery, many people thought I was living a normal life and fully functioning. But to my inner hub, and especially to Jim, I wasn't myself. I was not calm or peaceful, and I certainly did not exude joy. Externally, I was functioning, going through the motions on autopilot. Internally, I felt out of balance. My emotions continued their rollercoaster ride, as did my energy.

The truth was, I jumped back into my life at full speed and intensity. It was too much too soon. In the past, pushing harder was all I knew. Now, I couldn't. Something had to give.

I began by giving up Toastmasters and evening activities. Next, I gave up morning activities, so I could sleep in. Giving up my job or taking more time off was not an option at that time. Some women might have given up exercise. For me, giving up biking would have been like a death sentence, doing more harm than good.

I took a look at every single event, activity, and project in my life and asked myself a series of questions:

- Is this important to me?
- Is this important to me right now?
- Is this moving me toward my goals and dreams, or away from them?
- Is this something I can put on hold for a week, thirty days, three months?

As I addressed each item, I found ways to clear the extra non-essential items so I could make a space for healing, self-care, and balance. I'll discuss more ways to fix and optimize your spokes in Part IV.

Chapter 33: Food Triggers

I appreciate and enjoy a healthy relationship with food instead of one that is wrapped in a negative self-image, control, or self-soothing. I also know that at times, I fall into habits where food throws me off balance. Like many people, you may have food triggers that move you away more than toward your goals and dreams.

In *Transform: Building the Mindset to Change Your Body and Your Life*, I wrote

> *You may also have emotional triggers that cause you to binge eat or eat unhealthy foods. When your brain is too active, such as when you are anxious or tense, you can use food to numb yourself in an effort to slow down brain waves to make yourself more comfortable. On the other hand, if your brain is underactive and you feel bored or sad, food can be used to stimulate your brain waves to make you more comfortable. Sometimes, food helps you to feel full when your life feels empty.*
>
> *I eat when I'm bored, stressed, and anxious. I also eat when I'm not doing what I want to do or when I'm procrastinating. Discontent is my worst instigator for overeating. On the other hand, when I'm writing, gardening, or riding my bike, I am rarely thinking about food.*
>
> *Simple awareness of when and why you are eating can help resolve your emotional eating. If you feel hungry, start by drinking a glass of water and wait twenty minutes. You may be confusing*

thirst and hunger. During your wait time, check-in with your emotions to assess whether you are truly physically hungry, or if you are trying to suppress feelings of boredom, sadness, anxiety, or tension. If you start to notice that you eat when you are emotional, then try to resolve that emotion without relying on food. If you are bored, find something to keep you busy and take your mind off of food. Go for a walk, answer email, or clean out a junk drawer. If you are sad or anxious, consider talking to a friend or therapist. If you eat when you are tense, consider stress-reducing tools such as yoga, meditation, or deep breathing.

Alcohol, caffeine, and sugar can interrupt your natural energy and sleep patterns. Other foods to which you are sensitive or allergic can inflame you, causing discomfort and even illness or disease.

- **Alcohol:** Alcohol in moderation can be a large part of your lifestyle, especially when it comes to your social circles. I've had plenty of days where a cold beer or a glass of wine was my choice to reduce stress and unwind after a hard day or celebrate a victory or milestone or completed project. It is definitely a mood-changing drug.

  Alcohol can also increase my anxiety and disturb my sleep. And good quality and quantity sleep is a major spoke on my wheels to wellbeing. Being aware of this is essential every time I decide to tip a glass.

- **Caffeine:** Caffeine is another substance that can increase my anxiety and disturb my sleep. Anyone who has trouble sleeping will tell you: It sucks. While I prefer the all-natural route, there was a season of my life where I couldn't fall asleep or stay asleep, and I did resort to the use of a prescription sleep aid.

  What made the biggest, long-term difference was giving up my morning cup of "joe." It was not easy, but I was willing to give it up for my health and wellbeing. Relief did not happen overnight. It got worse before it got better, as my body slowly released this chemical from my cells. But over time the result was nothing short of miraculous and I was able to fall asleep easier and stay asleep longer.

  It took close to three weeks for me to feel the full effect of life without caffeine. But it had a drastic effect on my energy levels. I had always believed that caffeine gave me an energy boost, but the reality was that it was contributing to my fatigue. With each cup of coffee, I was borrowing energy from the future. The problem was, I was never replenishing it with rest and sleep, which left me frazzled, overtaxed, overwhelmed, and anxious.

  If you struggle with irritability, mood swings, panic, anxiety, anger, sleep disturbances (quality and duration), PMS, fatigue, depression, hormonal imbalance, headaches, gastrointestinal distress, or increased stress, then you might want to consider cutting back or eliminating caffeine altogether. You may find that as you do, your cravings for them decrease. Your energy improves, and you experience better digestion and sleep, and fewer headaches.

I was eventually able to add coffee back in, and it is something I continue to enjoy with moderation. You may find you no longer desire it or you may decide to add it back into your lifestyle. Either way, there's no harm in eliminating it for a few weeks to discover if life is better with or without caffeine.

- **Allergies and sensitivities:** In addition to common food depressants and stimulants like alcohol and caffeine, you may have food allergies or sensitivities. While my doctors did not find any specific foods I was allergic to, I discovered sensitivities to gluten, eggs, and whey protein.

If you struggle to feel good after you eat, live in your curiosity and work with your doctors, acupuncturist, or naturopath to discover if there are foods that are causing distress in your life. This one discovery could be the catalyst that helps you optimize your life.

Chapter 34: Stress

The crux of my underlying message with *Wheels to Wellbeing* is to find ways in your life to reduce stress so you can maintain your balance and increase your joy in life. That is why it is so important to know the spokes on your *Wheels to Wellbeing* as well as what causes your spokes to bend or break. Inevitably, stress is the biggest obstacle to many people's struggle to find and maintain their balance.

Chronic stress that goes untreated can affect the body, mind, and emotions. The accumulative buildup of stress has nowhere to go. It will make you sick and cause the bending and breaking of spokes to the point that you will crash. You will lose your joy, peace, relationships, presence, and purpose.

Stress can manifest when you lose hope or are not living up to your full potential. It shows up in the pain that comes from the death of a dream. It can appear when you are feeling too isolated or from not being part of a community or tribe.

If you are a type A high achiever, then rest is both important and tough for you. You strive, push, achieve, press, prove, and produce; it's how you're wired. Rest feels like a waste of time, yet your body craves it. Slowly, the accumulative effects of stress start to manifest in illness, anger, and frustration. You find yourselves burned out, overwhelmed, fatigued, and screaming at your kids, partners, loved ones, co-workers, employees, and friends. And then, a life event or change pushes you beyond your limits.

Our health is affected by the decisions we make daily. Stress is often not a result of one factor, but the cumulative effect of many factors. It helps to look at what you can control. You may not be able to leave a stressful job, but you can decide to be grateful and focus on the positive aspects of your work while looking for a career that is more aligned with your passion and purpose.

Life can get overwhelming. Rising stress levels are common. Many times, you know whether you have too much stress in your life or if you've been stressed for too long and something's got to give. Other times, stress isn't as obvious. It may be the result of an unhealthy relationship you've stayed in for too long, poor nutrition, too much or the wrong kind of exercise, not enough sleep, or any other number of reasons.

Stress indicators can include injury, headaches, cold sores, a change in your bowel habits, acne, muscular tension, tightness in your chest, interrupted sleep, weight gain or loss, fatigue, digestive distress, histamine issues or other illness or even disease. You may miss appointments or snap at loved ones.

Just because you don't feel stressed doesn't mean you are not putting too much stress on your body. If you are an athlete, you may be training with people better, faster and stronger. This is a great way to improve and challenge yourself. However, you need to know your limits, and build in recovery training and time. Or perhaps your job, finances or a relationship is causing subtle anxiety, which puts stress on your organs, emotions, and immune system. You may be planning a wedding or preparing for the birth or graduation of a child. You may be moving or changing jobs. You may be eating something that doesn't agree with your system, causing inflammation and physical stress.

So if stress is inevitable and everyone has it, how do you maintain a healthy lifestyle and optimize wellness? How do you reduce stress in your life and ultimately in your body so that you can live a healthy, balanced lifestyle? Learning about the prevention and optimization of your spokes will help, along with getting to know yourself, your strengths and your requirements to live a life of balance.

Part IV

Fixing and Optimize Your Spokes

DID YOU EVER FEEL LIKE something was off in your body? Perhaps your doctor ran tests and drew blood, only to tell you that everything's normal?

I don't know about you, but I don't want to feel normal. I want to feel exceptional. I want to live my life as abundantly as possible physically, mentally, emotionally, spiritually, financially, socially, and every way possible.

I don't want to barely get through my work day hating every minute of it. I want to create and build and inspire with passion and purpose and in service to others.

I don't want to live paycheck to paycheck, fearing I don't have enough extra to give. I want to have enough money that I don't have to worry about balancing my checkbook, or ask what it costs before I purchase something. I want to have financial peace and freedom to be able to give abundantly, and make a difference in the lives of those less privileged and fortunate.

I don't want to wander this earth alone, isolated and disconnected. I want to be fully engaged and present, socially committed and connected. I want the time and financial freedom to visit and vacation with family and friends whenever I desire; to be together to celebrate birthdays and anniversaries, baptisms and bar mitzvahs, first jobs and retirements, leaps of faith and crossroad contemplations.

I don't want to feel irritable or sad or anxious for no reason. I want my emotions to match the current situation; to be able to cry and mourn with compassion or cry and laugh in celebration.

To live life more abundantly, I want to prevent the bending and breaking of spokes and optimize every area of my life and overall wellbeing. So much of balance comes from knowing yourself and your spokes, as well as being empowered to rescue yourself from a life out of balance.

Chapter 35: Knowing When It's Time for a Change

Change is hard. Hard on us and hard on the people around us. One of the things that makes change so hard is that it is often unexpected.

In 2020, Covid-19 caused the world to face something new or unfamiliar every day. We were in uncharted territory that no one warned us about or prepared us for.

It was like that for me personally in 2015. One day I went into surgery to have an ovary removed, and the next day I woke up in sudden surgical menopause. I was 43 years old and my world shattered. Every aspect of my life was in turmoil.

As someone who tries to always look for the positive and the lessons to be learned from life, menopause was indeed a "pause." It was a wakeup call. It was a time to re-examine my lifestyle and self-care practices. It was a time to ask myself, "Are you living life more abundantly, on purpose, with passion and in service to others?"

At the time, the answer was no. I had no idea what my passions were, let alone my purpose. It had been a long time since I had given myself permission to dream.

Throughout that experience, I learned to live in my curiosity and turn inward. I started listening to my heart, and tuning out my overactive thoughts. Instead of looking externally for answers, I began to ask myself, "What is it that I want? Am I happy? Where are areas in my life I'm discontent? What's not working? What is?"

I didn't know exactly what I was looking for. But there were plenty of areas in my life where I said, "Not this. This is not what I want for my life."

During that difficult season, I turned my pain into purpose. At 46 years young I wrote my first book, *Come Back Strong,* and launched my career as an author. I wrote about my journey and all the tools I discovered that helped me find my balance. I wrote about overcoming setbacks and turning them into comebacks. The experience made me stronger, both emotionally and mentally.

Equally hard as unexpected change is the change that you initiate. You begin to exercise. You quit your job. You get married or divorced. You find a hobby like gardening, photography, or a ceramics class. Change could come from the commitment to remove toxic foods or people from your life.

When you initiate change, you may not have a clear vision of where you're going. You just know you can't stay where you are. When you are at that crossroads in your life, listen to that deep place inside you. You may not know what you want just yet, but you know what you don't want.

Honor the discontent. Acknowledge it. Embrace it.

Long before surgical menopause showed up, I dreamed of feeling calm and balanced. I dreamed of feeling healthy in my mind, body, and spirit. Long before I left an abusive relationship, I dreamed of a great love. Long before I left my job and life as an employee, I dreamed of time freedom and creating my own schedule in a career where my skills, gifts, and experience could be beneficial. I dreamed of a life where I was excited to get up each morning, confident that I was living out my purpose, and inspiring others to live a life of true health, love, laughter and freedom.

Life can be stressful and challenging at times. Maybe you're tired. You're not sleeping. You're exhausted from being overworked and underpaid.

If you are uncomfortable, in pain, angry, frustrated, and overwhelmed, if you are longing, wishing, hoping, dreaming of a better way and a life with more ease, you are not alone. You are not messed up. You are simply human. The best part of being human is that at any moment you have the ability to change. You have the ability to become the hero in your own life.

You may not know what you want. You just have to move in the direction of change. The remarkable thing about life is that changing one thing can be the catalyst for changing everything. It can be what sets you on a new path, in a new direction, toward those dreams and goals, toward a life of more passion and purpose.

For me, that change was getting healthy. It was saying yes when a friend reached out with a nutritional solution that allowed me to release weight, become badass on a bike, and transform my body so that it looked as strong as I felt.

That one change to my nutrition over twelve years ago was the impetus for me. Not only did I get healthy in my body, but I got healthy in my mind, my emotions, my relationships, my career, and my life. It was also a lucrative plan B from a financial standpoint, especially during the Covid-19 global pandemic. That year was tough on my family. My husband was a personal trainer and when gyms closed, that income stream went to zero. Later that year I was let go from a marketing job. Thankfully, that plan B was in place where we could pivot, change our focus, and put a plan in place to rebuild our finances. Regardless of whether you fear or embrace change, you can use it as a time to reflect, rebalance, and reprioritize.

Chapter 36: Take A Break

A balanced life requires—even demands—rest and recovery on a daily basis. You cannot wait for an annual or biennial vacation to take a break. Your health and wellbeing require time-outs on an annual, quarterly, monthly, weekly, and daily basis. This is where you take time to tune out the world and relax, play, and release the stress of everyday life. It is a time to rest, recover, reflect, and bring life back into balance. When your body is tired and your spirit weary, the best thing you can do is rest and recreate. Make this a regular part of your healthy lifestyle, not a quick fix.

Unfortunately, the motivation for change is often pain and heartbreak. It is in your struggles, when you feel out of sorts or when you suffer trauma, that you realize you are out of balance. When you feel irritable, sad, anxious, disconnected, or like you are striving more than thriving; when your list gets longer and longer, you binge eat, or self-medicate, or self-isolate, then it's time to take a close look and check in on the spokes of your wheels to wellbeing. It's time to slow down and take a break.

If you do not currently have built-in breaks or time-outs in your life, then the first step is to become aware of the signs that indicate you are in danger of bending or breaking a spoke. Revisit the section on "Sleep, Rest, and Recover" in Chapter 12.

Vacation and recreation provide time to heal, recover and restore. But there are other ways to take a break on a monthly, weekly or daily basis. Consider that acupuncture, massage, yoga, meditation, reiki and other energy work, and float therapy can be very effective at reducing stress and restoring your focus and energy.

A detox can also provide a physical break for your body that will trickle over into your emotional and mental health. Caffeine, sugar, salt, gluten, soy and dairy can all add stress to your body. A simple detox for several weeks will help you determine if certain foods are adding stress to your body. You can also give yourself permission to unplug or turn off your phone. Fasting from technology doesn't have to be long term. It could be at all mealtimes or between the hours of 8 p.m. and 8 a.m.

If you find yourself less focused, creative, friendly, or productive, it may benefit you to slow down or take a break. As your life comes back into balance, you will find you are able to come back stronger, more creative, productive, and refreshed, and with renewed energy and excitement. You'll have more passion for your career, relationships, and life in general. Overall, you'll feel more balanced.

Chapter 37: Self-Care Is Self-Aware and Intentional

As you proactively schedule in more breaks, you allow self-care to be intentional and habitual, instead of a reaction to trauma or overwhelm. You become more aware of what your body and life needs to feel more balanced. You give yourself more grace and love.

For most of my life, I lived by the philosophy: work hard, play harder. My order of priorities was work, and then play. Rest was simply not in my vocabulary. When challenges or obstacles came my way, I worked harder. If my body hurt or my soul was weary, I pushed through. Until I couldn't.

Maybe you can relate. I'm talking about those life events that add additional stress to a life you are already struggling to find balance with. It's an accident or illness. It's surgery or job loss. You find a lump. A friend moves. Someone dies. It's a heart attack. Cancer. Divorce. It's adjusting to a new way of working or learning. It's everything going on in our world including wildfires, racial and political tensions, Covid-19.

Often it takes a major life event to realize how stressed, overwhelmed, or out of balance you are. These life events force you to pause, reflect, and reprioritize. They force you to change and consider your self-care.

But self-care is easier said than done. You may not be so great at putting yourself first. Perhaps you create your to-do lists and figure you'll practice self-care when the list is complete (it never is). You take care of everyone else first, and when everyone's needs are met (they never are), you think of yourself. It's time to be more aware of and intentional with your self-care so that you can feel more balanced.

There is a story about rocks, pebbles, and sand that is used in time management seminars and teachings about priorities. You start out with an empty jar and a stack of rocks, pebbles, and sand. You're told all the rocks, pebbles and sand will fit into the jar, as long as you add them in the right order. Start with the wrong item and you will run out of room. Without awareness and intention, you focus on the wrong thing in the wrong order, and all the people, priorities and requirements of your life don't fit. You look at self-care like a piece of sand instead of the rock that it is.

One of the greatest lessons I've learned from setbacks and challenges is that when I make self-care a habit instead of a reward, I feel calm and balanced and more able to handle life events with more ease.

Self-care is about being aware of what builds you up, replenishes you, and restores your energy. It is knowing yourself and your needs and knowing what fills your cup, so that you can share joy and light and love with the world. It is all about knowing yourself and your spokes.

What activities drain you? Let those go.

What are the moments in life when you are completely engaged, relaxed, or happy? Do more of these.

Do you need solitude or connection?

Do you need to take a nap or dance out your frustration?

Some of my favorite forms of self-care include:

- yoga
- meditation
- quality time with my husband
- laughing with my sister
- riding my bike
- a walk in nature
- kayaking, paddleboarding, or simply being near the water
- fueling my body with good nutrition
- taking a nap
- enjoying a cup of tea with a friend
- relaxing in a bath with Epsom salts and essential oils
- reading
- writing
- dancing

Your list of self-care tools may look different. I have friends who run, ride horses, work out, and play volleyball as a way to unwind and reduce stress. Others paint, draw, sing, cook, dance, or pray. Many find joy with their dog, cat, or beloved pet.

Whatever self-care means to you, do more of it on purpose. Do more of what relaxes and recharges you as well as what brings you joy and laughter. The stuff that drains you? Find a way to do less of it. Add self-care to your schedule and make it part of the natural rhythm of your life instead of a reward, and you'll find that all your rocks, pebbles, sand, and everything else in your life simply fit.

Chapter 38: Checking Your Spokes

Wheels to Wellbeing is a tool for you to check in on a yearly, quarterly, monthly, weekly, daily, and moment-to-moment basis. It's a reminder to frequently ask yourself, "What's off? What needs my attention?" It's a tool to recognize a spoke that is beginning to bend and identify the cause. It's about being aware of your needs and emotions so you can respond more than you react.

When you are overcome with busyness, feeling overstimulated, relying too much on caffeine, alcohol, or sugar to self-medicate, or struggling with unresolved anger, angst, anxiety, or depression, then it is time to look closely at each area of your life and assess whether it is stress producing or stress releasing. Consider each area of your life, from your job, to your relationships, finances, passions, and purpose, and explore where you can make changes.

Before every bike ride, Jim and I check to see if our bodies and our bikes are in integrity. In simple terms, we make sure everything is working and operational like it was designed to function.

Have we fueled our bodies properly? Have we gotten adequate sleep? Are we hydrated? Did we recover from our last workout? Are we emotionally distracted? Do we have water and snacks with us? Do we have the right clothing for the temperature? Are we wearing our ROAD iD®?

To make sure our bikes are in integrity—have full workability—we make sure our tires are inflated properly, the chains are cleaned and lubed, and our saddlebags are equipped with what we need to service our bikes if we get a flat. We make sure we have working front and rear lights and water bottles. We run through our gears and make sure they shift properly and test our brakes. This checklist makes sure we do everything within our power ahead of time to prepare for a great ride.

You can create a similar checklist for your health and wellbeing. Listen to the subtle messages of your body...the aches and pains, the fatigue. Ask yourself: do I need coffee, water, sleep, fresh air, a bike ride, a hug, sex, or alone time? Sit in the quiet space between what you should do, and examine what you want and need to do.

Ask yourself:
1. Am I moving my body?
2. Am I hydrating my cells?
3. Am I fueling my life with the right nutrition for my body?
4. Are my hormones in balance?
5. Do I need more sleep, rest or recovery during this season of my life?
6. When was the last time I got still, and sought silence?
7. How am I feeling spiritually? Do I need to focus on prayer and meditation?
8. Do I have peace in my relationships?
9. Do I need support?
10. Is there someone in my life I can offer support to?
11. Am I present?
12. Am I being overcritical of myself? Where can I show myself more love and grace?
13. Do I need comfort from a pet? If I don't currently have one, can I volunteer and get my animal fix from a shelter?

14. How can I spend more time outside?
15. Have I rejuvenated at the beach, by the lake or an ocean, in the mountains, or elsewhere in nature?
16. Where can I build in more moments to dance or play?
17. Can I give myself a creative outlet through writing, music, dance or art?
18. When was the last time I laughed?
19. What am I passionate about?
20. What is my purpose?
21. How can I live my life in service to others?
22. Do I have peace in my career?
23. In what areas of my life do I have room to grow?
24. Is my schedule too full? How can I be less busy?
25. Have I taken a day, weekend, or week off lately? Where can I build in more breaks?
26. Are my vacations becoming staycations, where I work so hard around the house that I have to go back to work to rest?
27. Do I need to examine my diet or take a break from alcohol, caffeine, sugar or salt?
28. Do I need to unplug from the computer, phone, or social media?
29. How are my stress levels? What am I doing to reduce them?
30. How can I make self-care more intentional?
31. When was the last time I had a date night? Family day? Time with a friend?
32. When was the last time I got lost in a good book or a movie?

Chapter 39: Combining Spokes

As you consider all your spokes and areas of your life that need your immediate attention, you may begin to feel overwhelmed. Your wheels to wellbeing are not something you tackle or resolve overnight. Depending on how long you've been stressed, overwhelmed, or burned out, finding your balance may take weeks, months, or even years.

When you are out of balance, consider Wheels to Wellbeing as a tool: a way to honestly and intentionally look at your life and see where you can improve the quality of your life and optimize your happiness.

Some areas I've brought to your attention may not be of interest to you right now. That's okay. Re-examine your spokes in a year. Take time to assess them at key milestones in life and with each new season. This is a tool to make New Year's Resolutions and birthday wishes with more intention. It is a means to ask yourself, "Which spoke do I want to work on this year?"

You may be asking yourself, "How do I fit it all in? How do I live a productive life and find the time to manage each individual spoke?"

You don't.

You check in and assess regularly. You pivot when you need to. Sometimes you react and respond to whatever needs your focus and attention right now.

And you multi-task. You find ways to combine your spokes.

You only have so many hours in a day and so much to do, which can mean something important gets dropped. You schedule date nights, family time, and workouts. Then you try to work in socializing with friends, self-time, God time, and of course, work or producing time. All of a sudden, life is very full, or even over-full. This is one area where multitasking can come in handy.

Traditionally, relationships are built around food and drinking. Consider family gatherings and reunions. They often center on foods or holiday meals. Socializing at work typically means celebrating birthdays—with cake—or year-end parties or retirements or holiday events. All have a focus on food. When you get together for a girls or guys night out, it is often at a bar or coffee shop or lunch outing. Date night involves dinner or a picnic. And while prayer and meditation doesn't necessarily mean food, it often means being sedentary.

By combining your spokes, by interweaving relationship building with activities, your overall health and wellness will improve. You will be partnering and collaborating with the important people in your life and your inner hub while improving time management and making a busy life easier to manage. Check out the following examples and see where you apply these combinations to your life.

Building a relationship with God or your higher power or your spiritual side doesn't have to be done sitting or even indoors. My friend Scarlett begins every day with a walk up the mountain in her backyard where she communes with God. Nurture your spiritual relationship while walking, practicing yoga, skiing across an open field as the sun rises, or kayaking across a serene lake as the sun sets.

My husband led me to rediscover and rekindle my love of biking. Our date nights are often date rides. Some are fast, some involve hills, and some are long destination rides to see something new. For you and your great love, experiment with activities you can teach each other or learn something new together. Some ideas are biking, golf, kayaking, mini golf, hiking, or dancing.

Encourage the members of your family to move more. Make being active together fun. Consider family walks, a ride or run for charity, paddle boating or paddleboarding, relay races or team triathlons. As a child, my family enjoyed bike rides and canoe rides. Another family I knew did a team triathlon together.

My friend Janie leads a fun and vibrant life. Three days a week, you'll find her hiking up a local mountain with as many as five or six of her girlfriends. My friend Luna rises at 4:30 a.m. twice a week to meet seven of her girlfriends for a run before it gets hot. There have been times I've met two or three girlfriends at the gym twice a week. If you have enough friends, you could even join or form a soccer team. For a special treat, try trapezing or aerial fitness and performance.

If you work with a team of colleagues or co-workers, softball leagues are popular, as are charity events that involve walking, biking or golf. For those more adventurous, you could experience a team-building event such as a low or high ropes course. Grab a colleague and go for a walk at lunchtime. Talk to your HR department about their wellness programs. Their initiatives may pay for yoga, Zumba® or other fitness classes during the work day, lunch hour, or before and after the workday.

With life's demands, it is easy to forget about the important relationship with yourself. As much as your alone time can be in quiet and stillness, it can also be in activity and include walking, running, hiking, horseback riding, biking, snowshoeing, skiing, or gardening.

Above all, ask for what you want and be willing to create what you want. If you want to spend more time with family and friends, consider hosting a weekly Sunday brunch or Friday pizza night. Let people know you have an open-door policy where everyone is invited and there is always room for one more. Suggest they bring their favorite brunch item or pizza topping or beverage of choice.

Start a monthly supper club, book club, Bible study, wine or adventure or art and craft night for you and your girlfriends. Take turns picking the restaurant, meal theme, book, or activity. Invite people from your inner hub and outer circle to join you at a comedy club, take dance lessons, or do a quarterly neighborhood cleanup. Volunteer at an animal or homeless shelter or food bank.

There are so many ways to nurture relationships and combine them with the important spokes of your wheels to wellbeing, such as exercise, nutrition, play, the outdoors, dance, and service to others. Being present, finding peace, and laughing with intention are creative ways to think about building and celebrating the important relationships in your life.

Chapter 40: Be Aware of Your "Too's"

Watch out for the "too's" in your life. They seem to go in cycles. My husband's are very clear.

His first sign indicates that he is "too" tired.

Then he begins to feel "too" unproductive.

To combat that feeling he makes lists that grow longer and longer with each passing hour. This makes him "too" busy.

When he feels "too" busy" he quickly becomes "too" overwhelmed. Next up he becomes "too" exhausted.

Then comes "too" sick. So he stops everything and rests.

What he has learned is that rather than run the gamut of his "too's," which feels really bad, he can stop at the first "too." He can break the cycle. He can allow himself more rest at the beginning, when he starts feeling "too" tired and skip all those other exhausting steps.

Chapter 41: Know Thyself

Growing up, I had a built-in system to get my needs met. I had plenty of alone time in my room. I received comfort from my feline friends Mittens, Muffin, and Spaz. We had a pool in the backyard and a powerboat to enjoy on weekends and week-long camping trips, nurturing my needs to be outside and near the water. I had softball and soccer games where I could hit, throw, and kick. I could safely bike around the neighborhood, walk barefoot in my backyard, and run around a four-mile block. Even mowing the lawn was meditative. In my late teens and early twenties I worked mostly outdoors on boats and at a resort. There was a built-in network of self-care all around me.

In my mid-twenties, thirties, and forties I moved inside and away from those self-care practices. My technical, administrative and marketing skills developed. I became more responsible and productive.

And I became really, really tired.

I slowly moved myself away from the curious, playful, warm, whimsical adventurer I was. I told myself I could thrive in a fast-paced noisy world. I was strong, tough. I didn't need a break. I didn't need self-care. I used to fight the whole idea of slowing down. But beating myself up only intensified the energy and emotional crash that came from pushing too hard for too long.

Now that I'm approaching my fifties, I recognize that I am content, cooperative, and calm when I'm not overstimulated, worn out, or hungry. When I don't sleep or become overly fatigued, I lose my words and can't focus or communicate; I'm helpless to autocorrect. My body relies on me to take care of my basic needs: water, food, sleep, and movement.

All the personality tests pointed out that I was extremely introverted. However, I denied that part of myself, believing I was a practiced extrovert. Now I realize I just had better self-care tools in place.

For over two decades I jumped from job to job, vacillating between recreation and marketing positions where I was overstimulated, and administrative and web development gigs where I was able to hide behind a computer but which left me under-stimulated. During the first year of the global pandemic, I loved the isolation, and at the same time I was lonely. Did I become more introverted or did I simply lean into my introversion?

When I was 39 years old, I was recruited to a senior level marketing position at a beautiful resort 100 miles from New York City. It was a fast-paced, high-pressure, people-pleasing gig. At first I thrived, but quickly became overstimulated. As part of the application process, I took the Meyers-Briggs test. It was not my first time discovering that I was an INFJ: introverted, intuitive, feeling and judging. As such, I approach life with deep thoughtfulness and imagination. I care about helping and connecting with others, prioritize being kind and generous, and would rather cooperate than compete. Empathy comes naturally to me, and I prefer deep conversation to small talk. I am a sensitive soul. I enjoy having my own space and freedom. While I am creative, insightful and passionate, I am also sensitive to criticism, reluctant to open up, and a perfectionist prone to burnout.

Years after taking that test (and leaving that job) I met a woman who referred to herself as highly sensitive. When I asked her to clarify what she meant by that, her description struck a chord with me. She was easily overwhelmed by bright lights, strong smells, and loud noises. She needed to withdraw during busy days to a private place where she could recalibrate, refresh, and re-energize. She became overstimulated when a lot was going on around her, and excessive hunger disrupted her concentration or mood.

You can take a free test and discover more about yourself at https://www.16personalities.com/ and https://hsperson.com/. Why is this important? Because in knowing yourself, you can better learn what spokes you need to pay special attention to.

For example, one time I got so agitated and frustrated at a Super Bowl party, I had to leave early. The same thing happened at a convention where I was surrounded by a crowd of over 7,000 people that was super high energy and enthusiastic. The price for being around that is an emotional crash or low period. It's just my normal ebb and flow of life. I retreated to an exhibit outside the arena where I collapsed into a friend's arms in tears. She took one look at me and said, "Ah. Too much peopling. You're overstimulated."

I didn't understand what was going on with me at the time, but now I recognize that the noise and energy of a large crowd was overstimulating. There were multiple screens and conversations and music going on all around me.

While on a double date at a popular restaurant I became so disengaged from the conversation that my friend's husband picked up on it. He must have thought I was rude as I tuned into my own little world. It wasn't so much that I was disinterested in the conversation as much as I was overstimulated by the highly charged discussion of politics. Add this to the noise level and the fact that my back was to the room, so I was being bombarded with multiple conversations from other tables that overpowered the one in front of me. With all that stimulation, I was unable to be present, engaged and connected, something I truly value. Later that night we retreated to the quiet of their home, and I was much more comfortable and able to enjoy deeper conversations.

Knowing yourself and whether you are an introvert or extrovert—or something more, like a highly sensitive person or an empath—provides tools to cope and rebalance. Embracing who we truly are takes courage and hard work. But it can lead us from a life of struggle to one of strength. It can relieve anxiety and allow more room for empathy.

Chapter 42: Know How You Are Wired

When I discovered that I had a highly sensitive personality, I understood myself better and I felt less alone. I also realized that not everyone was like me. Apparently not everyone freaks out internally over the sound of the "Put your seatbelt on" alarm. Others don't leave the mall on Black Friday feeling traumatized, and need three days to recover. Now I realize that while I hate a crowded mall, it's not that I hate people or that all introverts feel that way; it was that I got overstimulated by the sounds, noises, voices, lights, signs, sales, babies, and emotions—especially if I had also been neglecting my other spokes.

While I am introverted, my husband is extroverted. We have different needs and different spokes. We are wired differently. Our brains operate differently. In addition, introversion and extroversion runs on a spectrum; some people are more introverted or extroverted than others.

I have run across many people who could not believe I was an introvert. They didn't see me as shy or anti-social. This is a common misconception. Introversion is not synonymous with shyness or social awkwardness. It's more about energy. Introverts get overstimulated and their energy wanes by being around people (especially large crowds) for long periods of time. They recharge by spending time alone. Extroverts thrive in a crowd, gaining energy from other people. They recharge by being social.

So I'm an introvert and writer. Jim's an extrovert who smiles at and talks to everyone. He thrives in a crowd and around people. I thrive spending time alone.

My internal battle is to be seen and, at the same time, to disappear. I long for connection but also want to be an invisible listener who is seen more than heard, until I have something meaningful to contribute. When Jim and I are around other people, it's easy for me to step into his shadow. But the world needs me to not disappear. I have insight and gifts to share. I am a mighty lioness who wants to roar as long as I can also retreat and seek cover, comfort, and safety under his wing when I feel overexposed and overstimulated.

When I get to this point of burnout or overwhelm, I'm tempted to shut people out. The more I know myself, the more awareness I can develop so that I can practice better self-care as a form of maintenance and prevention. I can take a walk, or find a quiet place, outdoors if possible. I can retreat to the bathtub for a quiet getaway. I can take a nap. Times like this I also need to be aware of triggers like caffeine that might add to my stimulation.

My friend has four kids and her house is always full, somewhat loud, and there are multiple conversations going on all at once. They all thrive in it and love it. The constant activity would overstimulate me. People walking in at all times would unnerve me. At the very least, I would need my own space to escape to. A safe haven that is calm and quiet and less stimulating. Boundaries would have to be set, including hours of operation. If the door is locked, text or call but do not enter. If it's open, you are welcome.

Know yourself and those people in your inner hub. Know how you're all wired. We're not the same. We all have different temperaments and mindsets. What's right for you may not be best for the people closest to you in your inner hub. If someone is an introvert, you can care for them by

- respecting their need for privacy;
- allowing them extra time to think or process;
- listening when they speak. don't interrupt or override them;
- giving them advance notice if you know change is coming;
- giving them time to finish what they are doing;
- not asking them to be more extroverted—their superpower is their introversion.

Likewise, if someone you love is an extrovert,

- respect their social nature;
- compliment and affirm them in front of others;
- be direct, not subtle or passive aggressive—they can't read your mind;
- allow room for spontaneity and adventure;
- don't ask them to be more introverted—their strength is in their extroversion.

Chapter 43: Stop Pretending You Don't Know

I used to want to be so mentally and physically strong that I could suffer through any experience. Now I want to be so peaceful inside that I can choose not to suffer when pain comes. I used to pretend I didn't know what I needed in my life to feel balanced. Now I periodically assess and address issues as they come into my awareness.

Take your family medical history, for example. Colon cancer is a predominant disease in mine. Knowing I'm at risk, I can do everything possible to keep my gut and bowels healthy. I can be proactive in getting colonoscopies, not out of fear, but out of recognition for what I may be predisposed to. I can pay extra attention to high stress, knowing that it compromises my immune system.

Periodically, take your pulse on your overall health. What is your stress level? Do you smoke? Are you overweight? Do you drink too much—alcohol, soda, or caffeine? These are all contributing factors to disease and illness that can bend or break your spokes.

Stop pretending you don't know you are at risk. You know what's going on. You know the state of your health. You know if you smoke, drink in excess, or over-caffeinate. You know if you need to cut back on sugar or salt. You know when you're self-medicating, chasing numbness. Words that hurt when you're sober don't bother you after a glass or two of wine. That feeling of being overstimulated is less powerful after a beer or shot or hit of cannabis. If you eliminate the things that make you numb, you have to feel all the emotions of your life, and they can be overwhelming without tools to rebalance.

You also know how stressed out you are. You know how long you've been stressed due to finances, your job, or relationships. You know if you are lacking passion or purpose in your life. You know if one or two spokes are bent or if all of them feel broken. Don't pretend you don't know. Nothing feels worse than feeling like a fraud in your own life.

Do more of what you love. Do less of what you hate. Do the work to fix your spokes and find your balance.

Chapter 44: Reduce Stress

To find balance and avoid burnout, you have to find ways to reduce stress. Here are a few suggestions:

- Make sleep a priority. It's non-negotiable.
- Add additional time in your day and week for recovery and repair.

- Add 15 minutes of free time to your morning and in between appointments.
- Plan your day the night before: meals, snacks, water, clothes, review your appointments and task list.
- Write it down. Have a daily task and checklist. What needs to happen for you to get out the door in the morning? Put it on the list. What has to happen before you can leave work? Put it on the list.
- Take a break—annually, quarterly, monthly, weekly, and daily.
- Exercise. Walk. Stretch. Practice yoga. Dance. Laugh.
- Create space to slow down.
- Manage your energy.
- Protect your calendar.
- Say no.
- Create boundaries.
- Do something you love every day.
- Perform an act of kindness every day.
- Compliment someone.
- Keep your thoughts and words positive.
- Guard what you let in: make sure what you read, watch, and listen to is positive.
- Switch it up. If you spend most of your day sitting, make sure you get up, walk around, or stretch at least once every hour. If you are on your feet all day, find a quiet spot to sit. Take a bath. Soak your feet. Or lay down for 15 minutes during the day or after work.
- Remove yourself from the stressful environment or walk away from the stressful person.
- Count your blessings.
- Speak your gratitudes out loud daily.
- Relax your standard.
- Turn off notifications on your phone and / or turn on the Do Not Disturb for set hours of the day.

Adaptogenic herbs are getting more and more press for being herbs that calm down your adrenals, the small glands that sit on top of your kidneys and help regulate your response to stress. Rhodiola, ashwagandha, schisandra, astragalus, and eleuthero root are a few of nature's ingredients that are considered adaptogens. They can help the body and mind recover from physical and mental stress and help you to maintain your balance.

Above all, connect with others. I find it easy to be alone. But I still need support, prayer, and love from other human beings. I need other superwomen in my life to remind me that we are all superhuman. That is the best way for me to reduce stress and offer myself more grace while living a more balanced life.

Chapter 45: Shake it Out

Soon after an animal in the wild suffers trauma they will shake to release tension and stress. This shaking or vibrating helps them discharge the negative energy, release muscular tension, burn excess adrenaline and calm their nervous system.[9]

While massage or talk therapy may help to reduce stress and tension, you may also benefit from working directly with the body and nervous system, similar to the way animals do. Health coach and trauma expert Adair Finucane, LMSW, says shaking therapy can be performed seated or standing. You focus on each body part, simply shaking it out. Finucane says that in as little as 10–30 seconds you can change the nervous system. Shaking can be done as part of daily maintenance toward stress relief or anytime you are feeling acute stress or trauma.

For additional support, you can look for a tension and trauma releasing exercises (TRE) provider. For more information or to find a provider visit https://traumaprevention.com/.

Chapter 46: Create a Safe Haven

For many years, the idea of creating a safe haven was rattling around in my brain. I envisioned something external, for other women—possibly for victims of child abuse or domestic violence. And while those areas are close to my heart, I eventually realized that it was me who needed a safe haven. A place to escape the noise and hustle and bustle of the world and recalibrate. A place to breathe and get still and quiet and reset. I needed a space where I felt grounded.

Sometimes this is a physical space: a quiet corner in your home where you can shut the door and tune the world out, even if for only a few minutes. It could be a quiet park bench in a noisy city, to which you retreat and no one knows your name. At work or in a noisy restaurant or conference, it's the bathroom. If you are an introvert or highly sensitive, you know what I'm talking about. I've met many of you hiding in the restroom, just trying to, well, rest. Perhaps that's why it's called a restroom.

For me it's multiple places. It's the quiet corner in my office. It's the bench next to the water. If necessary, it's on the underside of my eyelids, where I close my eyes, take a breath, turn inward, and remind myself I am loved. I am safe.

Safe from what? It's more like "safe to…." Safe to fall in love. To fall in friendship. To be vulnerable and truly seen. Safe to not have to weigh your thoughts or walk on eggshells around someone. Safe to take a break from busyness and noise and the chaos of the world, even the virtual one. A safe haven builds a buffer between you and everything else. It's a protective space that allows you to replenish your energy and feel more balanced in your world.

Chapter 47: Clear the Clutter

Jim laughs at me every time I do the dishes before starting meal preparation. I need to start with a clean slate. Dishes in the sink while I'm trying to prepare and cook a meal triggers my anxiety and discomfort. Clutter feels chaotic. It can deepen depression and leave you with a sense of overwhelm.

The more stuff I let go of, the happier I am. This was apparent in 2020. With the pandemic came the closing of our small private gym. We began selling and giving away equipment. We had talked about moving to the southwestern United States, but we didn't have a plan. We decided to "act as if" we were moving. With every sale and dumpster run, our world felt lighter. And when we settled in New Mexico, our goal was to keep clutter to a minimum. So far we have kept our promise to ourselves.

There are times when life feels chaotic and we don't know how to fix it. Sometimes we just have to start small and focus on clearing the clutter and chaos in our physical space. Clean out the junk drawer, the nightstand or your desk surface. Move on to a closet. Every day you flip through the clothes racks deciding what to wear. There are things in there that you absolutely love and others that you hate. They don't feel good when you put them on. Get rid of them. Donate or throw them out. Enjoy creating space in your closet; with that comes fewer items to decide between. Fewer decisions equals less mind clutter.

As you clear the clutter from your physical space, you end up with less stuff and more room to breathe. As you breathe deeper, you'll think and feel deeper. Life will feel more expansive and less constrictive or confining.

Chapter 48: Create a Space and Clear Your Plate

When I'm overwhelmed, I write out my list and I prioritize. What can I drop, delegate or postpone? What is out of alignment with my passion and purpose? Who has snuck into my inner hub who can be moved to my outer rim, even if temporarily?

During the summer of 2021 I was in a season of prolific writing and building an online system to sell directly to my readers. Everything else got postponed while I focused on two things: writing and learning how to set the system up—advertising, ecommerce, landing and sales pages, distribution, publishing multiple book formats, and automated emails. Blog posts, pitches to magazines, agents, and publishers, and website updates all got pushed to the side. I ignored social media and neglected housework. I removed all distractions in my mind to create the space needed to focus on one project, which in and of itself had multiple components to keep moving forward.

During times of extreme stress—such as when you or someone you love is diagnosed with an illness, has surgery, suffers job loss or promotion, gets married or divorced, moves, or in the case of a global pandemic—you may need to clear your plate until the dust settles and you feel like life comes back into balance. It is a time to learn to trust and not panic. Everything will still be there for you a day, week, or month down the road. This is the time to slow down, reflect, assess, and pivot if needed. It is a time to leave more margins and gentle transitions in the morning and evening. Give yourself an extra fifteen minutes before your work day or your commute, and do the same at the end of the day to make a list of priorities for the next day. It is a time to focus on the people in your inner hub, stay present, and find your balance.

Chapter 49: Just One Thing

Examining the spokes on your wheels to wellbeing works well when one or two spokes are bent or broken. It can also work when you are in a period of your life when all your spokes are broken.

Everything gets more intense during a major move, divorce, death of a loved one, job change, pregnancy, graduation, illness, marriage, or birth. At these challenging times, you need to prioritize and drop everything that is non-essential. Take a breath, and allow yourself to let go and reconnect with the present. Awareness of your breath brings awareness into your body, and to your self-regulating systems that work to bring homeostasis to the forefront.

Breathing is so automatic you forget you are doing it. However, when you tune in, slow down and deepen your breathing, you can refocus, calm your emotions and relax. Breath work can affect your cardio, brain, digestion, even your immune system.

From that breath you can focus on just one thing that you have to do at this very moment. This is not the time to multi-task; it's the time to push everything aside and do the one thing you require for your physical and emotional safety.

If you are in labor, the one thing to focus on is giving birth to a healthy baby. If you are in the midst of a divorce, the one thing you might need at this moment is legal or financial advice. Seek out an expert. If you have recently lost a loved one, the one thing you might need to move forward is time to grieve. If you are struggling with an illness your sole focus should be on healing.

Give yourself permission to do just one thing.

Chapter 50: Manage Your Energy, Not Your Calendar or Clock

Writing out your schedule can paint a clear picture as to whether you are out of balance. Track your activities for a week. Include exercise, work, a second job, hobbies, and activities. Include driving time, meal prep, and household chores. Are there areas you can cut back on or postpone? Can you work from home one day a week? Can you change a coffee date with a friend to a weekly walk? Can you delegate or hire someone?

You also want to ask yourself who is in your inner hub that deserves the best of you, the "you" who is high energy and fully present and focused, listening with compassion.

Often, people manage their calendar, filling up every vacant spot from before sunrise to well after sunset. I certainly did for decades of my life. After years of trying to be a Superwoman every moment of every day, I accepted the fact that I am human, with limited energy. The old way involved jamming things into a calendar. The new way clears a space to live with intention and be fully engaged and connect with loved ones while practicing self-care, and maintaining and optimizing my spokes.

There are days my energy abounds and I put six or eight or ten hours into a project. And, there are days where I don't have the physical or creative energy to put in any time at all. On these days I give myself permission to zone-out in front of the TV or get lost in a romance novel. After pushing for days and weeks, that's exactly what I need.

Some experts would advise me to write every day. I choose instead to follow the cycles of my energy, knowing that some days, the energy comes simply by putting my ass in the chair and beginning to write. But on the days when it simply is not there—my creativity or energy—I don't force it. I simply try again tomorrow.

Part of mastering this skill involves knowing your priorities and your purpose so that you can schedule things thoughtfully and with intention. It's learning to say no more often, especially to things that don't align with your health goals, purpose, passion, and priorities. Some weeks you can cross off the morning and evening hours on your calendar and schedule those as sacred "me" time. If you have an early morning Zoom call or yoga class, limit your activity that afternoon and evening. Plan on an afternoon nap or an earlier bedtime. If you have a late-night meeting or event, plan a slower, quieter morning the next day with a later start. When invited to add something to your schedule, ask yourself, "Is this something I really want to do? Does it align with my passions and purpose?" If the answer is not "hell, yes," then it is "hell, no."

Learn to monitor your days so that you don't burn the candle at both ends, rising early and staying up late. Look at your calendar and consider the week. Are you at the gym at 6 a.m. five days a week? Are you out of the house in the evening five or six nights a week? Is it all necessary? Where can you build in more rest and quiet time to reflect and replenish your energy?

Maybe instead of five early mornings at the gym, you can cut back to four. As you look at your weeknight obligations, ask if they fit with your passion and goals in life. If not, can you cut back or skip a few activities this week, or indefinitely? If they are important, you will find your way back to them.

Here are a few questions to ask yourself when you are reviewing your calendar:

- Do the activities on my schedule this week align with my goals and priorities?
- What activities are of the highest priority to complete this week?
- What activities are of least priority to complete this week? Can I postpone or delegate?
- This week, where can I build in extra time to rest and replenish my energy?

Chapter 51: Learn to Say No

Sometimes you are so busy that the things you do are no longer fun. Examine each obligation on your social calendar. It is perfectly acceptable to say no with grace and ask for a raincheck.

Women especially push and push, staying up late, getting up early. We don't rest. We work hard. We work harder. And when our schedule overflows, it is the yin activities, like yoga and meditation, that get dropped. Slowly, the accumulative effects of stress start to manifest in illness, anger, and frustration. We find ourselves burned out, overwhelmed, fatigued, and screaming at our kids, partners, loved ones, co-workers, employees, and friends.

And then, a life event or challenge pushes us beyond our limits.

Before we get to this point, we have options. Things we can do to restore our balance and better manage ourselves in time. One of the best things we can do is to learn to say no. Peace, health and balance are on the other side of "no."

When it comes to play, connecting, adventure, and trying new things, "yes" is exciting. That's not necessarily true when it comes to projects, committees, and more work obligations. Learn to set boundaries, simplify your schedule, and free up space. Remove yourself from a project or committee.

You say yes to projects and events because you never learned how to say no. Let me give you your first lesson. Repeat after me: "No, thank you."

That's it, really. You may modify it to "Thank you for thinking of me, but no I cannot do that" or "No thank you, that won't fit into my schedule right now."

And then, shut up.

Zip it.

Stop talking.

Really.

The tendency is to make an excuse, and as soon as you do that, it becomes a game and a contest over who has the stronger will. An excuse provides an open door for somebody (usually someone that you love) to convince you to say yes.

Two things I know:

1. Every time you say yes to something, you are making a promise and a commitment to someone else. What you have to ask yourself in the split second it takes to say yes or no is, does your yes come with a compromise to yourself, your goals, your family, or your health?

2. When you say yes to something you don't even want to do, you are disappointing yourself. And when you do that, you open the door to negative feelings of guilt and shame, which contribute to an increase in stress and can quickly cause one of your spokes to bend or break.

So the next time someone asks you to do something you know in your heart you don't want to do, pause. Take a breath. Smile. And say, "No, thank you."

Chapter 52: Rescue Yourself

As you develop tools to keep your wellbeing spokes in good working condition, you'll feel more confident and empowered. You'll give yourself more grace and space, for days without a to-do list and more fun.

You don't have to wait for cancer or heart disease or divorce or depression to dictate your balance and what you can do to optimize your life. You can set boundaries around your energy and time. You can do more of what excites you, and less out of a sense of guilt or obligation.

You can delegate more and take more breaks. You can take a leap of faith and follow your passion.

Some of you are waiting for your prince or princess to rescue you, in the form of a spouse, parent, or friend. You are waiting for your partner to come home and say, "Quit your job." You are waiting for a friend to confirm you are in a toxic or abusive relationship. You are waiting for some external event that causes or allows you to let go of something that is not serving you in life.

Getting unstuck or rebalancing your life takes courage. It is not always easy to say no to a project, but it may be essential. It's not easy to cancel a date with a friend, quit a job or leave a marriage. But sometimes it will be critical to your health and wellbeing to do so.

You know what you need to do to feel more balance in your life and to live life more abundantly, fully optimized. It's time you put a plan in action to rescue yourself.

Chapter 53: Beyond Your Spokes: When More Is Needed

You may need more help than what you can do on your own or what your support network of friends and family can provide. You won't be able to fix your spokes alone. You need more than a women's group or prayer meeting. You may require medical, spiritual, or psychiatric attention. Drugs may be prescribed temporarily or long term.

There is no shame in asking for or needing help. The world is changing, and conversations about mental health need to come to the forefront.

At my last job, I called in sick to take a mental health day. In advance. I notified the two people I thought needed to know, an office manager and the head of HR. Ironically, the woman from HR informed me I would have to take a personal day. I objected to this: isn't my emotional and mental health just as important as my physical health? I had never taken a sick day before, and I just wanted to give her advance notice to plan accordingly. Thankfully the office manager chimed in and said sick days were for physical or mental wellbeing and did not need to be scheduled in advance.

In the last decade we have read about and watched as celebrities and professional athletes have struggled with pressure and overwhelm. As recent as the Tokyo Olympics, athletes took a break to restore their mental health.

I have known family and friends who struggle with anxiety, depression, and bipolar disorder. It is no longer something to hide or sweep under the carpet. It must be brought into the light. As we learn more about tools that can help people with these challenges, we have access to more tools that help us find balance and optimize our health and wellbeing.

Chapter 54: Balance Will Find You

As you bring balance to your awareness, you create space just for you. To go to bed early and sleep late. To take naps. To get back to a consistent practice of yoga and meditation. To get still, seek the silence, rest, relax and recreate.

I'm still in the process of learning how to plan for balance as best as I can, knowing there are two strong parts of me, the social, outgoing adventurer and the quieter, sensitive introvert.

What does that look like? As a speaker or presenter I am required to bring my A game, my high energy and show up as my badass self to bring a message that will inspire women. The time leading up to an event like this will be full, busy, stressful, and at the very least, a lot of hard work.

It will also require me to build in quiet time before and after so that I can maintain my balance and restore my energy. Beforehand, I consciously clear my schedule. I create a space to get in alignment with my passion and purpose. I meditate, relax and play more. No early morning or late-night activities or events. Instead, the focus is on meditation and yoga and breathing and extra sleep. After the event, I will require extra rest, play, and recreation.

I am still learning how important balance is to a healthy lifestyle as well as to a productive and purposeful life. I know that if I don't build balance in and focus on my self-care spokes, then balance will find its way into my life in the form of fatigue, irritability, weight gain, insomnia, headaches, apathy, and burnout. And I'll never live an optimized life if I am not balanced and operating at my best.

Chapter 55: From Pushing to Peace

One of my life's goals is to continue to ride my bike in beautiful places around the country and the world. Regardless of where I ride, there are always ups and downs. There are some roads that require effort, and others that allow me to coast. When I'm flying downhill with the wind in my hair and a smile on my face, I focus on the ease of moving forward. When I'm riding in a paceline I take advantage of the draft, knowing that if I'm in the second, third, or fourth position behind the lead riders, I'm riding with much less effort. Even when I'm climbing uphill, I can choose to speed up my cadence and put the effort in my lungs, while giving my legs a break, or I can stay in a higher gear and keep the effort in my legs, while giving my lungs a break. If I move around in the saddle, I can shift the strain from my quads to my glutes. And if I'm on rolling hills, I can use the terrain to speed up going downhill, so that I can coast further uphill with less effort.

Life is the same way. There are times you coast and times you climb. During my surgical menopause, Jim's prostate cancer diagnosis and surgery, and our move across the country, it felt like the climb would never end. But we eventually reached the peak, and there came a time to coast for a while and catch our breath, while enjoying the view.

Coast when you can. Find as much ease as possible, even as you do the things that aren't easy. Live and work in a way that makes you resilient for the long haul.

From my early days of bike riding, Jim coached me on the concept of "burning matches." When you burn a match, you have pushed yourself to your physical limits. At the start of every ride, you have a full box of matches. But once you burn them all, you are done. Every effort where you attack a hill or go all in on a sprint, you are burning a match. We all have a different number of matches. The smoother your ride, the more ease you allow and the more efficient your ride, the longer your ride can be.

Remember some of the earlier tools that will allow you to bring more ease into our life:

- Delegate.
- Ask for help.
- Take a break.
- Know thyself.
- Do just one thing.
- Clear the clutter.
- Manage your energy more than your time.
- Learn to say no.

Some jobs from my past had me on a dangerous track. I gave the best of myself to my job, neglecting my inner hub. The tender inner core of my life and home were stretched beyond their healthy limits. Jim got neglected. Sleep and sex and play and cycling got neglected. Relationships suffered. I suffered. I was headed for a crash when I lost touch with my essential self, Jim, friends, and family.

In the beginning these jobs were exciting and exhilarating. But they quickly led to exhaustion and overwhelm. It was overstimulating. This caused me to seek a slower-paced job that required less energy, which left me under-stimulated. The rollercoaster ride called my career left me always seeking balance. And independence. And the ability to create my own schedule, which fortunately, I'm now able to do. There were times I worked my ass off for other people and hated every minute of it. Now, I get to work my ass off for myself and my family, and I love every minute of it. I push when I need to, coast when I can, and make sure I leave time each day for peace and rebalancing.

Sometimes you are in a season of our life where you can't slow down. If you can't remove obligations, you can choose to do things with ease. Focus on relaxing. Release the struggle. Change your mantra from "Life is so hard" to "I do all things with ease."

Allow yourself the joy of the downhill. To stop. Rest. Take a break. Look around. Breathe. Connect. Simply make eye contact with another human being, and then, smile.

Does your business require a lot of phone time? How long are your phone calls? Can you cut them in half? Let people know at the beginning of the call how much time you have. Set a timer and get right to business.

Social media has many benefits and it can be a major distraction and time stealer. Set a limit per day and use a timer. Stick to it.

One email or negative post first thing in the morning and the day is off to the wrong start. At the very least, your brain gets activated and puts you into work mode before it needs to be. Guard your mornings. Ease into your day with loved ones or in pleasant solitude. Refuse to check email or social media before a certain time. Make sure it's not the first thing you do when you open your eyes.

In the past I thrived with the thrill of being a workhorse, worker bee, and linebacker. I worshiped at the altar of my to-do list, ignoring the cry of my body and soul.

Now, the best thing I can offer the world is not my force but my well-tended spirit, my wise and brave soul, and my calm energy. For me that requires no more pushing, or rushing. Only less. Less stress, less crying, less wine, less noise, less busy. And more. More dancing, laughing, playing, resting, connecting, presence, self-care and self-love. More peace. More living with passion, on purpose, and in service to others.

I wish the same for you.

Notes

1. Craig Groeschel, *Chazown: Define Your Vision, Pursue or Passion, Live Your Life on Purpose* (Colorado: Multnomah Books, 2006, 2010), p. 101.

2. Lyn-Genet Recitas, *The Plan, Eliminate the Surprising "Healthy" Foods That Are Making You Fat—and Lose Weight Fast* (New York: Grand Central Publishing, 2013), p. 45.

3. Josh Axe, "Top 15 Anti-Inflammatory Foods and How to Follow This Diet," Dr. Axe (accessed July 31, 2021), https://draxe.com/nutrition/anti-inflammatory-foods.

4. Biote Medical accessed August 4, 2021, https://www.biotemedical.com/

5. Haanel, Charles F., The Master Key System (accessed August 3, 2021), https://www.thefreemasterkey.com.

6. "The Benefits of Recreation," City of Richmond, British Columbia, Canada (accessed August 16, 2021), https://www.richmond.ca/parksrec/about/mandate/benefits.htm.

7. DiSalvo, David, "Six Science-Based Reasons Why Laughter Is the Best Medicine," *Forbes* (accessed August 2, 2021), https://www.forbes.com/sites/daviddisalvo/2017/06/05/six-science-based-reasons-why-laughter-is-the-best-medicine/?sh=b2be1047f04f

8. Shawn Achor (accessed October 23, 2017), http://www.shawnachor.com.

9. Vinall, Marnie, "Can Shaking Your Body Help Heal Stress and Trauma? Some Experts Say Yes," *Healthline* (accessed August 2, 2021), https://www.healthline.com/health/mental-health/can-shaking-your-body-heal-stress-and-trauma

Resources

Website
www.LoriAnnKing.com

Books By Lori Ann King
Come Back Strong: Balanced Wellness after Surgical Menopause

Transform: Building the Mindset to Change Your Body and Your Life

Courses by Lori Ann King
Balanced Wellness During Menopause

Books by Jim and Lori Ann King
Raging Love: An athlete's Journey to Self-Validation and Purpose

About the Author

LORI ANN KING is on a mission to inspire you to live a life of true health, love, laughter, and freedom. She is the Amazon best-selling author of *Come Back Strong, Balanced Wellness After Surgical Menopause*, and a two-time contributor to the Chicken Soup For the Soul series.

Lori is a cyclist and was a runner for over twenty-five years, competing in races ranging in length from two to 26.2 miles. She is a 2019 IsaBody Challenge Finalist and 2017 IsaBody Honorable Mention. She has an undergraduate degree in Recreation from Western State College of Colorado and an advanced certificate in Information Management from Syracuse University.

When she's not writing, you'll find her with her husband, Jim on their bikes, paddleboards, kayaks, or in the gym.